The Bridge to School

The Bridge to School provides concise, targeted information for teachers who work in PreK, Transitional Kindergarten, or Kindergarten settings, covering both the why and the how of play in classrooms, along with insights into how the normal development of 4-to-6-year-olds is manifested and how teachers can harness and work with those typical needs and behaviors. This powerful professional resource includes theories of child development, brain development, and the value of play-based learning, but the majority of the content is practical classroom strategies that fall in line with ECERS and allow for appropriate academic skill building.

Claire Bainer is Co-Director of BlueSkies for Children, an NAEYC Accredited program.

Liisa Hale is Co-Director of BlueSkies for Children, an NAEYC Accredited program.

Gail Myers is a bilingual teacher and literacy coach for K–3.

Other Eye On Education Books Available from Routledge
(www.routledge.com/eyeoneducation)

Better Lesson Plans, Better Lessons
Practical Strategies for Planning from Standards
Ben Curran

Your First Year
How to Survive and Thrive as a New Teacher
Todd Whitaker, Madeline Whitaker, and Katherine Whitaker

Dealing with Difficult Parents, 2nd Edition
Todd Whitaker and Douglas J. Fiore

Teaching ELLs to Read
Strategies to Meet the Common Core, K–5
Paul Boyd-Batstone

Infusing Grammar Into the Writer's Workshop
A Guide for K–6 Teachers
Amy Benjamin and Barbara Golub

Empowering Families
Practical Ways to Involve Parents in Boosting Literacy, Grades Pre-K–5
Judy Bradbury and Susan E. Busch

Get Organized!
Time Management for School Leaders, 2nd Edition
Frank Buck

The Bridge to School

Aligning Teaching with
Development for Ages Four to Six

Claire Bainer, Liisa Hale,
and Gail Myers

Routledge
Taylor & Francis Group
NEW YORK AND LONDON

First published 2018
by Routledge
711 Third Avenue, New York, NY 10017

and by Routledge
2 Park Square, Milton Park, Abingdon, Oxon, OX14 4RN

Routledge is an imprint of the Taylor & Francis Group, an informa business

© 2018 Taylor & Francis

The right of Claire Bainer, Liisa Hale, and Gail Myers to be identified as authors of this work has been asserted by them in accordance with sections 77 and 78 of the Copyright, Designs and Patents Act 1988.

All rights reserved. No part of this book may be reprinted or reproduced or utilized in any form or by any electronic, mechanical, or other means, now known or hereafter invented, including photocopying and recording, or in any information storage or retrieval system, without permission in writing from the publishers.

Trademark notice: Product or corporate names may be trademarks or registered trademarks, and are used only for identification and explanation without intent to infringe.

Library of Congress Cataloging-in-Publication Data
A catalog record for this book has been requested

ISBN: 978-0-415-78957-8 (hbk)
ISBN: 978-0-415-78958-5 (pbk)
ISBN: 978-1-315-22264-6 (ebk)

Typeset in Bembo and Gill Sans
by Saxon Graphics Ltd, Derby

We dedicate this book
To those who taught us,
To those we teach, and
To those they will teach in turn.

Contents

Meet the Authors		viii
Preface		x
Help! Index		xii
1	How Children Learn to Learn	1
2	The 3R Framework: Room, Routines, and Relationships	31
3	Guiding and Growing the Whole Child	73
4	The Art of Teaching Self-Control	120
5	Language that Supports Young Children	139
6	The Bridge from Play to Instruction, and Instruction to Play	160
	Appendix 1: Typical Patterns in Development from Ages Four to Six	180
	Appendix 2: Play-Based Learning that Supports Academic Success	186
	Appendix 3: Suggested Additional Reading or Viewing	190
	Glossary	191

Meet the Authors

Claire Bainer has been the Co-Director of BlueSkies for Children, an NAEYC Accredited program, since 1995. She received her MA in Early Childhood Education at Mills College. Claire has taught in preschool classrooms and at the college level for 40 years. Her years of classroom experience strongly inform her adult teaching, weaving the interplay of classroom and family dynamics with academic theories of development and mental health to explain the art and science of effective teaching for young children. Claire has been a fellow of LeaderSpring, chaired the Early Mental Health Systems Group as a member of the Alameda County Child Care Planning Council Steering Committee, and served on the Oakland Mayor's Education Cabinet, the Early Learning Advisory Council for Alameda County, and the U.C. Berkeley Early Childhood Education Programs Advisory Committee.

Liisa Hale has been the Co-Director of BlueSkies for Children, an NAEYC Accredited program, since 1995, and has 35 years of experience as a teacher and director in full-day programs for children under 5. She leads workshops for teachers and parents about meeting the needs of young children, as well as teaching directors how to manage quality early childhood programs. She served for 12 years as a California State Director Mentor, two of those years with the intensive Every Director Counts Project of Alameda County First Five. She holds a BA in Early Childhood Development and Education from Mills College.

Gail Myers has worked with every age group from 2-year-olds through sixth grade during her career in education. She worked for Hayward Unified School District as a bilingual teacher, a literacy coach for K–3, and a language arts intervention teacher in the upper grades. She has also been an instructor and coach for both preschool and transitional Kindergarten teachers at BlueSkies for Children in Oakland. She has trained many groups of teachers on topics such as working with English Language Learners, Child Development, and Preschool Curriculum, as well as workshops for parents. She received her BA and Early Childhood Teaching Credential from Mills College, and her MA degree in Early Childhood Education from San Francisco State University.

Other collaborations of Bainer, Hale, and Myers:

Gail, Claire, and Liisa have collaborated in the production of these teacher training videos and study guides: *Foundations for Relationship: Quality Infant Care* (2013), *Literacy in the Preschool Years* (2010), *Beyond the Curriculum* (2003), and *Growing through Play* (1991), filmed by videographer Ray Enriquez. Claire and Liisa co-authored *Second Home: A Day in the Life of a Model Early Childhood Program* (2007, Redleaf Press) which is accompanied by a DVD directed by Gail and filmed by Ray.

Preface

The differences between 1-year-olds and 2-year-olds, or 2s and 3s, are dramatic and clear. But 4-year-olds do not look that different from 5-year-olds. Fours and fives walk, talk, climb and, to varying degrees, listen and get along with others, which can easily lead to asking 4-year-olds to do what 5-year-olds do. But in fact neuroscience tells us that 4s are working with less mature brains, which process information and learn in different ways than the brain of a 5-year-old. A growing number of 4-year-olds are being served by programs with public funding under a variety of names and frameworks—Universal Preschool, PreK, Transitional Kindergarten, Early Kindergarten—but in many cases the teachers and administrators in those programs need more information about the learning style and capacity of younger children.

This book is designed for teachers working with this transitional age group from 4 years to 6 years of age, providing a combination of developmental theory and practical techniques that will lead to success for the teachers and the children in their classrooms. For simplicity, we use the term **PreK** to refer to 4-year-olds whether they are in a preschool or elementary school setting. **Kindergarten** refers to 5-year-olds and young 6-year-olds.

We include child development theory to provide insight to behavior, because a teacher can work more effectively with behavior when the reason behind it is understood. This will be new information for many teachers in K–12 systems, while those coming from the preschool world may skip over it or use it as a refresher about how to work with development to reach teaching goals.

The chapters roughly align with the course of a school year, beginning with a little research and theory to set the context then diving into the concrete details of how to set up a classroom and systems that support the children's learning through both guided play and teacher instruction. Later chapters go into greater depth, exploring the reasons behind common behaviors and the ways young children learn, and providing effective techniques to work with them. We know that teachers always have long and pressing lists of things to do, so we have also made it easy to look up one topic in the Help! Index—new art ideas, or how to help a child who can't stop crying—and just read that piece right now.

We hope you will want to continue learning about teaching young children, and invite you to the BlueSkies for Children website for more resources, www.blueskies4children.org/.

Claire, Gail, and Liisa

Help! Index

Quick references for the top ten topics requiring urgent answers.

Topic	Page
Strategies for aggressive behavior	125–38
Hitting	122–5, 128–32
Biting	129, 132–3, 139
Strategies for a crying child	134–5
Strategies for an anxious child	90
A child who swears or uses "bathroom talk"	144
Time out? Try the Quiet Corner	127
Discussing sensitive issues with parents	67–9, 136
Working with volunteers	58, 69–71
New ideas for the art center	42, 104–11, 163–4
Using circle time to build community	134, 168–9
Explaining play-based learning to doubters	26–30

Chapter 1

How Children Learn to Learn

Key Information in this Chapter
- Brain development and its effect on the child's learning styles and abilities
- Why play enhances classrooms and learning for young children
- Developmental needs and capacities
- The teacher's role in orchestrating an effective balance of play and instruction
- Explaining the learning in your classroom to parents and colleagues

Our mature, educated adult brains have ideas about how we go about learning. If we are pursuing an academic subject we do research or listen to lectures. If we are learning how to fix a car, we might read but we will also find a good mechanic to demonstrate techniques, answer our questions, and then guide our practice. If we take up golf we might watch videos and hire a pro to coach us as we learn to drive and putt; the coach may also suggest we work on foundational skills like balance, strength, and coordination. We have many strategies at hand, and can pick and choose the best ones for each job.

Yet when we began life we could only learn by taking in a random assortment of information through our senses, and could only communicate by crying. Neuroscientists now know that brains reach full maturity around the age of 25, two decades after children typically enter Kindergarten—and still, babies learn most of their strategies for learning in the first five years of life. Dr. Alison Gopnik says "We learned most of what we need to know a long time before Kindergarten. As adults we can survive in our particular world because as children we figured out how it works."[1] How is it that this immature brain moves in just five years from a single strategy for getting its needs met—crying—to the multiple competencies of formulating its needs or ideas into a cohesive thought, expressing that thought in words, taking in the reaction of others to those words, then responding by modulating its first thought and articulating a new one? Typically, children all over the world develop all these skills without "study" or "lessons"—they learn by watching and listening to people around them, copying behaviors they see (like the aspiring mechanic), practicing the words they hear, and receiving coaching in the challenging moment from the pros in their lives—adults and older children.

For 100 years observant teachers have known that young children learn best when they are in the company of competent, caring and responsive adults who guide and support, but only occasionally direct, the children's activities. They have seen that when children select their own activities—which the adult labels as play—they work hard to achieve their goals and learn more as a result. Teachers also observe that if children set goals that are too challenging they comfortably reframe them so they can be achieved with self-esteem intact. Teachers of babies, toddlers and preschoolers learn as part of their teacher education how to set up effective, intentional, constructive play. Yet even though we know now from neuroscience as well as observation that this is the best way for children to learn, most teacher preparation fails to include this vital information.

The trend in education has been to ask 4-year-olds to act like 6-year-olds, as if they are no longer governed by the rules of biology and development. Rather than honor the learning style of 4-year-olds as something different than that of 6-year-olds it has simply been labeled inadequate. As children grow from the pre-Kindergarten age of 4 they are still learning the most from their own self-directed play; by the time they enter first grade around age 6 they are beginning to learn other ways to learn. What is it that children need to learn when they are 4 or 5, and why is it more effective to teach it through play than through lessons?

Defining and Valuing Play

While everyone has an idea of what the word "play" means, in the world of early education it refers to a very specific type of activity. When we say "play" we mean an activity that is:

- freely chosen,
- self-structured, and
- self-directed.

To be **freely chosen**, there must be a multitude of options available; doing a puzzle is freely chosen if a child had the option of puzzles, blocks, dollhouse or books, but it does not meet the standard if every child in the room was told "now do a puzzle." To be **self-structured** means the child (or a group of children in agreement as they become cooperative players) decides how to approach the activity; if she can start her jigsaw puzzle any way she wants, maybe constructing the dog in the middle first, it's self-structured, but if she is told she must start by putting the straight edges together it is not. To be **self-directed** means the child is in charge of the experience, and will change it to suit his own learning capacity and the relationships he has with others.

When the teacher directs the children's activity, even if they are using play materials like blocks or balls or tempera paint, it fails to meet this definition of play.

Throughout this book any reference to play is based on this definition. Children "self-teach" through free play on the playground at recess—there is a growth opportunity every time a group decides to play hopscotch and needs to negotiate turns and rules—but greater growth comes with the teacher's guidance when she has selected play materials that will advance the children's skills and understanding in specific areas she has identified, and where she can step in with a timely comment that supports or expands the play and the child's understanding of how to interact with other people in his world. Chapter 2 will delve more deeply into this concept of Guided Play.

The learning that comes through play is hard to measure but is a foundation for life skills just as much as academic skills. It is easy to measure whether or not a child can count to 10—but the ability to count to 10 is just rote recitation with little value for a child who does not understand one-to-one correspondence, or that 8 represents more of something than 6 does. It is easier to count the number of letters that a child can name than to measure whether he can listen to a story and grasp its content—but naming letters is only a small piece towards the big goal of enticing a child into the vast world that lives in stories and books.

It can sound like contradictory advice to be told to "teach through play" and at the same time be told not to direct the play. How does one teach through play without telling a child what to do? The best way to visualize this is that the teacher *guides* the play, by putting out materials that will elicit the kind of play that she wants to see and by adding information or materials as the play develops. For example, if she wants the children to learn to talk to each other in the dramatic play area she will put out props that support interpersonal relationships—dolls and dishes, office supplies and keyboards, toolboxes and steering wheels. (She will not put out light sabers, because she knows that they are likely to lead to fighting play rather than friendly conversation!) As she sees children picking up the toolboxes and steering wheels she can step back if they are happily sharing ideas to make cars out of the blocks and drive on a camping trip. But if she notices that they pick up those items and then seem short of play ideas she may just happen to come by and say "Uh-oh, is your car broken?" Suddenly the children have a framing idea and as they begin to embrace it and plan their play the teacher can step out again. Subsequent chapters will provide the teacher with many more strategies to guide play.

Research Supporting Play-Based Learning

In the 1970s Germany experimented with shifting from its play-based Kindergartens to early learning centers that focused on cognitive achievement. When they compared the children of 50 such Kindergartens with those in 50 play-based Kindergartens, they found that:

by age ten the children who had played excelled over the others in a host of ways. They were more advanced in reading and mathematics and they were better adjusted socially and emotionally in school. They excelled in creativity and intelligence, oral expression, and "industry." As a result of this study German kindergartens returned to being play-based again.[2]

Daniel Goleman's 1995 book *Emotional Intelligence*[3] broadly introduced Americans to the concept that mastery of what are now known as "soft skills" predicts life success more accurately than test scores or grades. Goleman cited multiple examples of people with high cognitive intelligence and test scores failing to achieve as much as others with only average intelligence, but with stronger interpersonal skills. Understanding people, he argued, was perhaps more important in managing one's life than high scores in academic exams. In fact, high intelligence without some sense of self-awareness and ability to control one's impulses interferes with personal success—a child who requires instant gratification will choose to play a video game rather than study for tomorrow's test, sometimes leading to academic failure despite high intelligence.

Once again, for many generations observant preschool teachers had been quite sure that this was true, but they lacked the science to prove it and lost ground to policy-makers pushing brain-focused, teacher-led instruction to younger and younger children. Since the early 1960s there has been a growing cascade of proof that success has a lot more to do with self-control, self-esteem, social skills, flexible thinking, curiosity, creativity and strong executive function in the brain than it has to do with innate intelligence; once a child has those pieces in place teaching math and reading is easy. In addition we have learned that 4-year-old brains really are biologically not ready to learn through the same methods that work for most 6- or 7-year-olds.

Summaries of the Research

- The "marshmallow test" in the 1960s by Stanford University psychologist Walter Mischel. In this experiment, the adult left a 4-year-old in a room with a treat on the table in front of him, saying the child could eat it if he wanted—but if he would wait until the experimenter returned then he could have two marshmallows. Dr. Mischel found in follow-up studies that children who could delay gratification at age 4 earned significantly higher scores on their SATs when they were seniors in high school!
- The Perry Preschool project.[4] In 1962 the HighScope Perry Preschool Program out of Ypsilanti Michigan identified children from low-income homes deemed at risk for school failure based on environmental factors

and low IQ scores. Half the children attended a play-based half-day program taught by well-educated preschool teachers for two years. The lives of these children have been followed for **40 years** along with the control group who did not experience guided preschool play, with reports periodically issued about their progress in life. The researchers were a little disappointed when they evaluated the children after the first few years of elementary school, as the differences between the two groups of children were quite small. However, each successive round of research, conducted in five-year intervals, found the quality of life of the Perry Preschool participants diverging more markedly from the children in the control group. By age 40, the study found that those who had been enrolled in the Perry Preschool had higher earnings, were more likely to hold a job, had committed fewer crimes, and were more likely to have graduated from high school than adults who did not have the play experience in preschool. Compared to the control group:
    o At the age of 5, over twice as many Perry Preschool children tested with an average IQ or higher.
    o At the age of 10, less than half as many Perry Preschool children had been held back a grade or placed in Special Education.
    o At the age of 15, three times as many Perry Preschool children mastered basic achievement tests.
    o At the age of 40, the Perry Preschool children were more likely to have graduated from high school, attended college, earn a living wage, or own a home. They were less likely to have been arrested, become pregnant as a teen, or have lived in a relative's home as an adult.
- Since this study, several others have found similar or even stronger results (e.g., the Abecedarian project out of Chapel Hill, North Carolina in 1972 and another project out of University of Chicago).
- The HighScope Preschool Curriculum Comparison Study (PCCS)[5] explored more deeply the relationship between a preschool where children learned through self-initiated play and later success. Another group of low-income "at risk" children was assigned to three different preschool programs—one was a Direct Instructional program with teachers giving scripted lessons and asking the children for correct answers, one was play-based with traditional nursery school activities guided by teachers with a background in child development, and one used the HighScope curriculum featuring child-initiated activities but with a "plan, do, review" system. Again, the initial outcomes for all three groups were not dramatically different. By age 23, however, those in the Direct Instruction group were 8 times more likely to have needed

> Special Education and 4 times more likely to have been arrested for a felony. Measuring 17 variables, the study concludes that the time spent in self-initiated activities in preschool "seems to contribute to the development of an individual's sense of personal and social responsibility."
> - A study of Federal Preschool Development Grant[6] PreK programs that failed to produce school success found that in those programs the children spent 27 percent of their active time in transitions (waiting to do something), 25 percent of their time with the teacher instructing the whole group, 16 percent working in "centers" (perhaps play, but more likely an instructional activity), 8 percent in gross motor activity, 3 percent in small group instruction and 2 percent in special activities (the balance of time was devoted to naps and meals). These programs clearly did not trust self-initiated play as a viable learning strategy, and as a result the public invested considerable funds with no gain in outcomes for the children.
> - The Dunedin Multidisciplinary Health and Development Study[7] found that the ability of a 3-year-old to control his behavior strongly predicted good health and financial security at the age of 32; conversely, the 3-year-old who struggled with self-control was more likely to have had financial difficulties, substance abuse, unplanned children and a criminal record by the age of 32.

These studies all confirm that the best way to teach the brain of the 4-year-old is to give him the opportunity to learn about himself and the culture to which he is born—and the best way to learn that is not through instruction, but through guided play. Once again we hear from Dr. Gopnik:

> Even in cultures without 'official' schooling, there has always been an implicit understanding that teaching three-year-olds is different from teaching six-year-olds. Throughout cultures and historical periods, only the older children have seemed suitable targets for formal instruction, in everything from the catechism to needlework to the protocols of knighthood.

Is there an age where the switch flips and a child is ready for more instruction? According to Dr. Gopnik, it is after the age of 5 that children "know about knowledge and how learning works."

Brain Development and Typical Behavior

Teachers have many strategies to engage the curious, active mind of a young learner. One of the most useful tools a teacher can have is to understand the typical trajectory of a growing brain, and the way that its assimilation of new information predictably affects the child's behavior. This allows the teacher to anticipate the child's readiness, responses and reactions as the teacher scaffolds learning and extends the complexity of play. Each area of development influences the development of the others, and allows all areas to work together, influence each other and create capacity for subsequent growth in every area as well. This interrelated growth in all domains strongly influences how the young child learns. For example, it is obvious that a child with speech delays will struggle to express his needs but, in addition, his social skills will lag because it will be hard for him to engage with the other children, and his brain will not be adding the neural connections that use speech to develop the upper cortex.

Knowing how the growth of the brain and body interrelate and influence the ability to assimilate and process information is a very important piece of successful teaching in the early years. Our social and cultural norms may change quite quickly, but human evolution is slow and follows the same sequence it has for centuries.

Growth is Not Always Comfortable

The brain's development predicts behavior; each time the brain reaches a new stage of understanding the adaptive process follows a similar pattern of questioning followed by assimilation.

As the child's physical growth and experiences in the world feed the brain, neurons connect more and more areas inside the brain, which supports more complex thought, which increases understanding. In this process the children must experiment to see if their new ideas are consistent and trustworthy before they can accept them, and subsequently change their behavior and understanding of the world and their experience in it. In their immaturity, this experimenting may be disruptive. When children are working to understand conceptual change and assimilate new ideas into their worldview it is common for them to test adults and limits; it is as if children's subconscious minds say "Well, now I see that I was wrong about all these things I thought I understood, so I wonder what else has changed?"

Children test their new hypotheses in ways that are consistent with their own temperament and growth. Children with limited language test in more physical ways (have tantrums, hit, throw and break things); children with more language test verbally (argue, complain and sass). Not only do they need to revisit all their old beliefs to see if they too have changed, they may also feel confused, fearful or frustrated. When the stage resolves with a new expansion of understanding, it is accompanied by a process of emotional integration and harmony. Children under 6

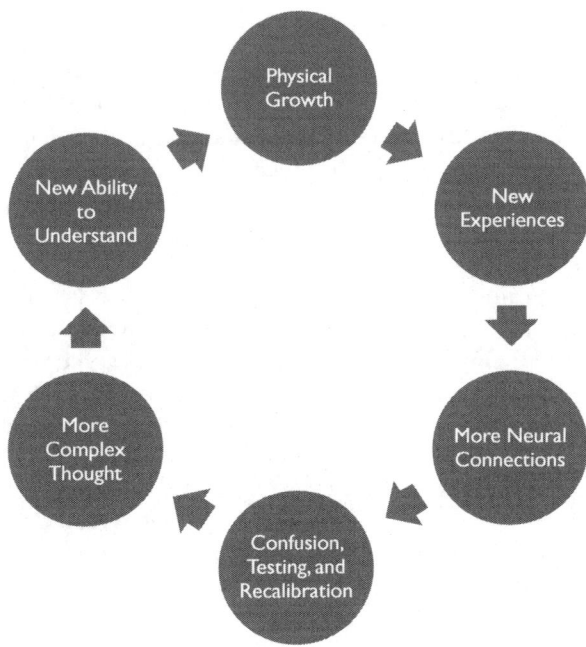

Figure 1.1 The cycle of brain growth—intake, assimilate, and expand

experience very rapid brain growth, so these big conceptual changes and physical changes happen many times over the course of a year. This requires considerable adult support, guidance and compassion; imagine how unsettled you might feel if every few months your arms and legs changed length, your beliefs changed, and your understanding of how things and people behave changed!

Between 5½ and 6½ years the growth slows and conceptual changes in understanding occur more or less annually; while the body continues to grow it is now similarly proportioned to that of an adult, making the internal relationships of the body more stable. While we can estimate the typical sequence that development will take, and can place markers of ages near stages, we also acknowledge that development is influenced by many factors. For example, children who have spent most of their time with adults prior to school will still pass through the typical stages of play with peers that they missed; first they will do what a 1- or 2-year-old does, then what a 3-year-old does, and then what the 4-year-old does, regardless of their actual chronological age. The difference is that older children enter each of these stages with a more physically mature brain so they can progress through each stage quite a bit more quickly. With this brain capacity in place, the concepts and understanding will "catch up" when exposed to the needed experiences.

Brain growth is not a choice made by the child, nor is the behavior that accompanies it. Remembering this helps us feel patience and compassion for the child in the throes of a difficult stage of growth. Every increase in a child's intellectual capacity creates doubts and anomalies in the child's understanding, which force changes in the child's behavior. A well-known example in development is that of 2-year-olds; the toddler's egocentric belief that his beloved adults are some sort of extension of himself is repeatedly contradicted when those adults set undesired limits. The child proceeds to test the adults until he understands whether he is an extension of the adults he loves or an autonomous and separate being with his own free will. This child *must* resist compliance whether he wants to or not, until he can gather enough data to be convinced that he can stop testing and move to the next stage.

From age 4 to age 6 another profound transition occurs, recalibrating the child's relationship with the world she lives in. Similar to the transition in the second year of life, this two-year transition also reflects dramatic brain growth, physical development, and cultural assimilation. In these two years the child's sense of self takes a profound leap, her thinking moves from the literal and concrete understanding of the world to the somewhat abstract, and the child's level of personal responsibility becomes more reliable and accountable. Following the familiar pattern of brain development the 4-year-old begins sensing that things are not as she thought they were, which brings profound testing—testing that is often embarrassing and unpleasant for adults, as the areas tested at this age go to the core of our cultural belief structures. Kindness, compassion, respect, and obedience all come into question as the child experiments with social norms and external vs. internal control. Happily, this uncomfortable stage leads to the positive outcome of stronger self-control and ability to manage in a group of peers with less adult support between the ages of 5 and 6.

Four-year-olds are intrigued and tantalized by the confidence and abilities they see in the bigger children around them, and also realize they are still young and vulnerable and cannot keep up. They see that soon they will be expected to manage their own lives, away from family, among these awe-inspiring big children, and be responsible for their own actions. There is good reason for 4-year-olds to anticipate, worry, and test. One can expect a normal, healthy young child in this transitional window to behave somewhat outrageously; in fact they must, to progress to the next stage of development. They brag and boast and boss, and delight in being out of bounds and naughty. They take glee in doing things to upset others, and love seeing this behavior in their peers as well. All this behavior is their testing as they practice being big in goofy, inappropriate ways so they can figure out how to fit in and actually behave in (relatively) socially successful ways. They are developing more sophisticated language, impulse control, and social or cultural awareness, which requires them to increase their own emotional control. This is a huge conceptual transition in the child's understanding of himself and others and his society. All these feelings bring up more social testing, defiance and even physical aggression as they try to make sense of the changes so they can learn to conform to the new social expectations.

These typical stages of behavior were originally studied and named based on close external observation of thousands of children; more recently we have learned that the reason those behaviors are so sequential and predictable is because they accompany and mirror typical brain growth and development.

Why Kindergarten Starts at 5

Development builds on itself, so a successful 5-year-old needs to have had the opportunity to be a highly functional 4-year-old; to become a functional 4-year-old the child must have had the opportunity to be a wonderful 3-year-old, etc. Human beings cannot skip stages in their biology, although as noted above children with gaps in their development due to lack of opportunity can catch up very quickly in the right setting with skilled support. The interplay of individual children's experiences with the growth in their brains and bodies are all interwoven with biological development. Chronological ages do not always correspond to developmental age; a 4-year-old who has had little interaction with peers will behave more like a 3-year-old in social settings until some experience and adult coaching help her catch up. A child who acts younger than her chronological age does not want to be annoying or difficult, but simply has not developed the understanding and skills that will allow her to conform. It is the teacher's job to help with that.

Four-year-olds seem big and competent, commonly deceiving adults into thinking that they are not that different from 5-year-olds. But while 5s are known for their developmental equilibrium, 4 is an age famous for the **dis**equilibrium described above—non-conforming, brash, challenging and out-of-control. The behavior of 4-year-olds, and especially 4½-year-olds, needs strong adult support and coaching, particularly around social interaction. This is the culmination of the drive from ages 3 through 5, when children are trying to understand the world through very external and concrete investigation as they do not have enough abstract thought to turn over complex ideas in their heads. They actively initiate and create social experiences to explore. They want to know how people get along with each other, who is in charge of what, and whether or not they can be in charge (especially if they beg or make promises or threats!). They explore cultural norms by being rude and inappropriate to see what happens when they make others—especially adults—uncomfortable, embarrassed, sad or mad. Play is a very effective medium for learning all those lessons during this external period. Whether they are rolling playdough, climbing monkey bars, building with blocks, or planning a birthday party in the dollhouse, the children can act out and explore all of the questions they have about getting along with people among a group of others who are also figuring it all out.

Hurting each other's feelings with classic "You can't come to my birthday party" behavior, rolling around being silly at group times, or using inappropriate language are ways that 4s learn about people's feelings and learn to manage their own behavior. Four-year-olds are diligently working to manage and express their big feelings, and learning to listen to others' feelings too. They are testing to find out what happens when they indulge their natural egocentricity and what happens when they have the capacity to exercise generosity of spirit. They learn that nobody will play with them when they are rude or won't share the Legos, which gives them an incentive to learn to take a breath and stop themselves before they alienate their peers. These experiences provide much more meaningful consequences than irritating a teacher or parent. When early academic instruction replaces play-based learning, 4-year-olds are not able to fully explore and complete this not-always-charming-but-oh-so-necessary stage of development.

Learning that happens during play gives children opportunities to learn to control their impulsive behavior, to be reflective, and to take responsibility for their actions. Listening to an upset friend who doesn't want to play anymore (because you got so excited you stepped on his hand while building a race track with blocks) has powerful consequences. It also gives teachers opportunities to coach children in self-control, empathy, and model or help the child develop appropriate language. This individualized teaching, when aligned with each child's developmental process, frames the adult's role as that of coach and helper. The teacher helps the children as they play to know what is expected of them, what to do and what to say to get along with others, and even how to notice where their bodies are. In this process the teacher can clarify and address the testing behavior, effectively lessening it and shifting potentially negative experiences to positive ones. When the child's initiative—including the inevitable mistakes—is constructively and positively framed, the child becomes more and more purposeful and positive in his interactions.

This is all foundational work that gets children ready to be part of a class group. Given the sequential nature of development, children who come to Kindergarten without having sorted out these questions or having had social experiences are developmentally driven to work on their social development, to the detriment of any academic agenda the teacher might have in mind. Unfortunately it is usually also to the child's detriment, for she will likely be in trouble for exhibiting normal (annoying) developmentally appropriate behavior that she actually needs to grow through now that she has the opportunity.

Kindergarten in the traditional structure with its requirements for conformity can be very difficult for typical 4- and 4½-year-olds, especially if they are also new to the experience of being in a social group of peers. This is why a PreK classroom provides a better fit for children under 5, as well as for 5s with little or no group experience. These younger children simply have not achieved the level of development that allows them to do what their older peers can easily manage. Starting school at 4½, during a stage of emotional disequilibrium, before most children have matured enough to shift from seeing themselves as individuals to seeing themselves as part of a group, before they are interested in conforming or pleasing adults, before they physically have the ability to sit still for long, or hold a pencil well, or think with the abstraction needed to succeed in Kindergarten, is setting the child up to struggle, dislike learning and dislike school. It also sets up teachers by making their work more difficult and less effective than it would be with children who are ready for academic instruction.

This is why Kindergarten works best when children start at age 5 rather than the age of 4. Five is typically a sunny, compliant stage of developmental equilibrium, an optimal time to undertake the challenges of Kindergarten and its new behavioral expectations. It is smooth for the child, the parent and the teacher. What a difference a year of development makes! Children who feel confident in themselves as both individuals and part of the social group are now ready to learn more academically—in fact, they can hardly be stopped. The emotionally and socially grounded child who has been hearing stories, and watching adults write things down, and whose brains and eyes are able to differentiate letters, will be constantly asking adults to help them read every bit of print they come across. Just as the developmental drive makes a baby want to walk, and a toddler ask why, and the 4-year-old treat people badly, the developmental drive makes us want to learn as soon as we understand what academic learning is about.

Two seemingly contradictory truths are always evident in teaching: development is individual and every child is unique—and at the same time development is predictable and full of recognizable patterns. Good teaching techniques easily transfer from one child to another because they flex in alignment with the brain's development and the child's unique personality. Understanding how predictable development drives behavior, and recognizing those patterns, will assist the teacher in choosing the right support at the right time for each child. She will understand when play will be the best vehicle to support the child's learning forward, and when the child is ready for more adult input and direct teaching.

Readiness for Success in Elementary School

It seems logical that the way to prepare children for school would be through doing school-like activities with them. However as we have established, the PreK brain that is getting ready for school is not the same brain that will be arriving in the Kindergarten classroom. Thus the way that children get ready to do well in elementary school is by building healthy bodies, brains that are primed, eager and inquisitive, emotional stability and social proficiency. Alphabets and numbers and colors are easily learned in the context of playing to build all this foundational capacity. The National Education Association (NEA.org) offers the following list of suggestions to parents about helping their children be ready for Kindergarten:

Preparing Your Child for School

What is School Readiness?

It is never too early to start providing the kinds of experiences that will help your child enter school ready to succeed. "School readiness" refers to the academic knowledge, independence, communication, and social skills children need to do well in school. Getting your child ready for school requires you to spend time reading, talking, and playing with your child.

Academic Readiness

Before entering Kindergarten, children should have basic knowledge of themselves, their families, and the world around them. Through play and interactions with caring adults, children can come to school with many skills that teachers can build upon. To **get your child academically ready for school, you should**:

- Read to your child daily and talk about what you've read.
- Visit the library. Check out books and attend story times.
- Sing rhyming songs and do finger plays.
- Put your child's name on their clothing and toys to help him or her recognize their name in print.
- Encourage your child to write his or her name.
- Help your child learn basic colors by pointing and naming objects like "green trees," "red apples," or "blue coats."
- Give your child puzzles and games that require counting and problem-solving. Let your child scribble, draw, write, and cut and paste.
- Sing the Alphabet Song with your child and provide letter magnets or other toys that will help him/her begin to recognize the letters of the alphabet.
- Take your child to the zoo, park, grocery store, post office, and pet shop. Talk about the sights and sounds of your day.
- Make time for your child to sing, dance, climb, jump, run, and ride tricycles or bikes.
- Choose child care that promotes learning with well planned, fun, and interesting activities.

Social Readiness

Social readiness is as important as academic readiness. Being able to get along with other children, follow directions, take turns, and say "good-bye" to parents are skills that Kindergarten teachers hope to see from incoming children. To **get your child socially ready for school, you should**:

- Set rules and give consequences for breaking them.
- Have regular routines for mealtime and bedtime.
- Encourage your child to play with and talk to other children.
- Encourage your child to take turns and share with other children.
- Encourage your child to finish difficult or frustrating tasks once they have begun them.
- Encourage your child to consider the feelings of others.
- Model and discuss positive ways for your child to express his or her feelings.
- Discourage hitting, biting, screaming, and other negative behaviors.
- Kiss and hug your child several times a day.

Independence

When children complete basic self-help tasks such as zipping their coats or tying their shoes, they feel a great sense of pride. Independence builds confidence and self-esteem. In school, children will be expected to do many things on their own. To **make sure your child is independent in school, you should**:

- Buy shoes and clothing that are easy for children to buckle, zip, and fasten on their own.
- Let your child get dressed and put on shoes by him or herself.
- Encourage your child to take turns and share with other children.
- Let your child do simple chores like setting the table at mealtimes or cleaning up toys after playing.
- Encourage independent toileting and hand washing.
- Let your child work independently on activities such as completing puzzles.

Communication Skills

Listening and speaking are the first steps to reading and writing in the preschool years. Through conversations with parents, teachers, and friends, children learn about the people, places, and objects that they will later read and write about. It is through speaking that young children tell us what they know and understand about the world. To **make sure that your child can communicate his or her thoughts and feelings in school, you should**:

- Have regular conversations with your child.
- Encourage your child to listen and respond to others when they speak.
- Answer your child's questions, even if the answer is "no."
- Help your child learn and use new words.
- Explore language through singing, rhyming, songs, and chants.
- Model the language you want your child to use.
- Write notes to your child.
- Help your child dictate letters to family and friends.

Children in high quality, play-based PreK programs enjoy most of these experiences in their day at school as well as at home. Early childhood educational specialists understand that the way to prepare children for an academic career is not through worksheets or lectures, but through play, young children's most effective mode of learning. This is why the play-based groups did so much better over the long term than the Direct Instruction group in the HighScope Preschool Curriculum Comparison Study (PCCS) cited above; the children in the Direct Instruction group were not learning how to learn, but how to comply with an adult's requests even though it had no context in their brains. This was also true in the Federal Preschool Development Grant study, where the children spent most of their day waiting for something to happen or being told what to do.

What is more, by the age of 10 it is impossible to tell whether a child learned to read at age 4 or age 7. Trying to turn Kindergarten into "the new first grade" is not only unnecessary, but even worse it begins a cycle of failure for the many children who are not developmentally ready to read at age 5. Sebastian Suggate of University of Otago (New Zealand) says:

> One theory for the finding that an earlier beginning does not lead to a later advantage is that the most important early factors for later reading achievement, for most children, are language and learning experiences that are gained without formal reading instruction. Because later starters at reading are still learning through play, language, and interactions with adults, their long-term learning is not disadvantaged. Instead, these activities prepare the soil well for later development of reading. This research then raises the question, if there aren't advantages to learning to read from the age of five, could there be disadvantages to starting teaching children to read earlier … In other words, we could be putting them off.[8]

16 How Children Learn to Learn

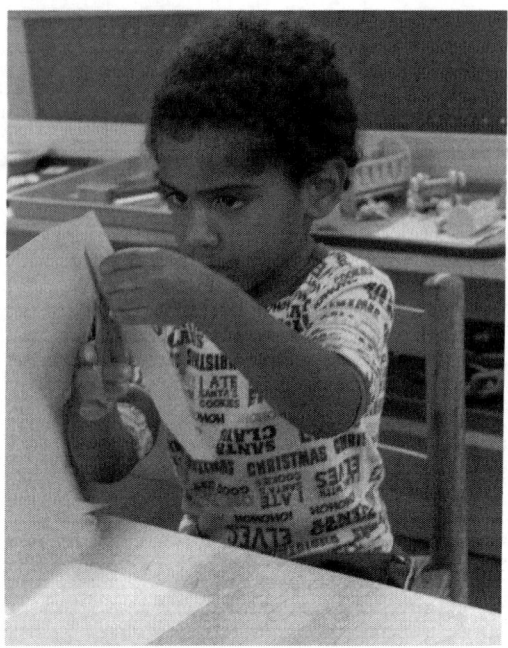

Figure 1.2 Developing focus, concentration, hand–eye coordination, and small motor skills
Source: Photo courtesy of Geraldine Rocha.

Indeed, trying to teach 4-year-olds to read is not only commonly frustrating but also robs them of a year to develop qualities such as managing impulses, self-regulation, delaying gratification, developing executive function—the foundations on which a child's success builds.

Trusting Time and Growth While Providing Opportunities

Child Development was one of the first cross-disciplinary fields of study; early in the 20th century theorists and researchers from the fields of biology, pediatrics, social work, nursing, education, psychology, and anthropology all contributed their insights to the development of young children to create the knowledge base which informs this work. Now contributions from the discipline of neurobiology add another dimension to our study of young children.

Developmental theorists like Piaget, Erikson, and Vygotsky have focused on different facets of children's growth, and described growth patterns in different ways, but share a broad agreement that growth is a function of both the child's genetic, biological structure and the child's environment (both the people and things around him), and that children mature through certain predictable stages in the same order, but not at the same rate.

These principles remind us that neither parent nor teacher can manipulate development, as it is determined by the child's inner clock and life experiences, but she can most certainly manipulate the environment to offer optimal support and encouragement for the child's learning. Besides the physical environment, she also controls the curriculum, the daily schedule, her own interactions with the children, and she can strongly influence the children's interactions among themselves. She plans the experiences they need to develop verbal skills, symbolic thinking, social skills, self-control, and personal responsibility. The rich environment provided by the teacher allows children to build on their strengths and uncover their innate talents.

These principles provide a framework to describe the typical balanced and whole development of young children. In the early years, learning emanates from the child. She constructs knowledge from the physical and social experiments that she tries out during play and through her everyday relationships. Thus the supportive adult creates an environment that gives the children a place where their actions and experiments with things and people will build, lead to questions, rebuild, and solidify understanding of their world.

The teacher makes her classroom a safe place for children to try these experiments, and gives the students the language they need to express their ideas and communicate with the other children. The teacher is also a model of how inquisitive, caring, and knowledgeable adults approach problems and cooperate with others.

Most of all, the teacher trusts that development will follow its prescribed pattern; her job is to determine where the child is on the developmental continuum and keep him moving forward. She trusts that a child who cannot yet see the difference between "d" and "b" will get there, maybe at age 4 and maybe at age 6. In the meantime she needs to keep that child swinging on the monkey bars as well as using fine motor skills with scissors and Legos—all of which will develop motor skills and the hand–eye–brain coordination that precedes reading and writing—and protect his self-concept from being bruised by curriculum that he is not yet ready for.

The teacher with a clear understanding of the developmental continuum, who trusts that the child will mature with the right support, can accept and enjoy the child as he arrives in her classroom. Rather than be frustrated by an immature child, or challenged by a bored child, she sees that her role with every child is to support him along his personal developmental trajectory towards the achievable goals that she sets for him. She stays fluid in her thinking, knowing that an immature and inexperienced child will always progress best by going back to the younger stage and mastering it before progressing to the stage expected in his age group. If a child has not completed a stage in his development, for whatever reason, his brain has still continued to grow, so assimilation of missed knowledge can be quick. This kind of developmental delay will easily disappear, allowing the child to catch up with ease, as long as someone notices and addresses it. This beginning, learning how to learn, is so foundational that even if a child can be made to achieve a desired goal without back-filling the gap, it will always leave a shaky foundation for future learning. This is what happened to the children in the PCCS study who were giving "right answers" instead of playing when they were 4.

When Not to Trust Time and Growth

We have established that every child learns at his own pace, but in a developmental program it is still important for teachers to recognize when that pace is significantly out of sync with the class group. Children with special needs often profit the most from early intervention, so the teacher must learn how to "trust development" while also watching out for a child who needs extra support, or a specialized type of education. Generally a child whose developmental stage lags more than a year behind that of the other children in the class will profit from additional intervention. However, as we mentioned at the beginning of this chapter, children at the age of 4 or 5 may have had very different experiences prior to arriving in the classroom. Some have been home with a loving grandparent or nanny and had little experience as part of a group. Some have been in disorganized group care settings where the children learned that being loud and aggressive will get one's needs met. Some have been in programs with a strong social-emotional component, who can express their needs and expect others to do so as well. It will take the teacher some time to get to know each child and determine whether they simply need some time, experience and coaching to align with the rest of the group or whether there is some other developmental need in play. Most teachers find that after working with a child for about three months they will either see significant learning progress or they will request assessments by specialists such as the school psychologist or learning resource teacher to be sure nothing is missed.

More than once in this chapter we have referred to the need for physical maturity and experience along with "the right support" to help children develop. What is "the right support"? That is what the rest of this book is about—how a developmentally attuned framework of support leads to meaningful learning.

Both Play and Instruction Are Important

One of the many misconceptions about a play-based classroom is that the teacher never instructs the children, but "just lets them play." Teachers know that children need grown-ups to help them, and they also know that the lessons the children will learn best are those that rise out of their own experience. The trick lies in balance and timing—this is what makes teaching an art as well as a science. As children learn to play in a group, with toys that elicit their own ideas, the teacher is busy teaching them systems and routines, as well as how to come up with an idea! Chapter 2 goes into depth on the topic of routines, along with the other structures that launch a successful school year. The first direct instruction that a teacher does is usually teaching routines—teaching the children where to put their jackets so

How Children Learn to Learn   19

Figure 1.3 Co-existing play and instruction
Source: Photo courtesy of Monaire Taylor.

they can find them at recess, how to paint at the easel without muddying the colors in each paint cup, what to do so the pieces don't get lost when you put away an uncompleted puzzle.

In the course of the day there are many opportunities for the teacher to offer instruction, but they must be addressed as they arise rather than come from a schedule on the wall. When a child asks the teacher how the snail he captured in the garden can move without feet, the teacher must recognize her opportunity to show how to use the library—finding the book about snails, and reading the page that explains how they move along a mucous trail. On the other hand, if the child is sitting and raptly watching the snail munch on a leaf, the teacher might choose to leave him alone to pursue his own thought train for that moment; she knows that putting a book in front of his nose would be replacing his perfectly legitimate learning agenda (scientific observation) with hers. And in a third scenario, if many children in the classroom are fascinated by snails this spring, and hunting under every leaf to find them, the teacher might present some larger group lessons about snails by reading the entire snail book at story time and helping the children chart out unanswered questions they have for future research. She might put materials to build "snail houses" in the art area and initiate some discussion about what snails need to live. Here the teacher is helping the children "know about knowledge and how learning works" which comes to most children, Dr. Gopnik says, around the age of 5. There is much more on this topic of "Emergent Curriculum" in Chapter 6.

In the Emergent Curriculum model the teacher follows the lead of the children, knowing they are going to learn the most if she fits her teaching into their interests. At what point does she begin to stop following and take leadership of the learning? One of the best ways to know that children are ready is to compare their development with expectations of Kindergarten readiness:

Kindergarten Readiness

(A summary from the National Educational Goals Panel)

I. Physical Well-Being and Motor Development
The child is physically fit, has good stamina throughout the day, effectively uses senses to take in information, has well-developed gross motor skills (balance, run, climb), uses fine motor skills (cut with scissors, hold pencil, manipulate small pieces), able to care for own physical needs.

II. Social and Emotional Development
A child who has developed a positive sense of well-being will demonstrate the emotional security necessary for successful interactions with peers and teachers. Able to express feelings, exhibit prosocial behavior, bond, cooperate, negotiate, assert needs but also listen to others' needs.

III. Approaches to Learning
Positive attitudes, habits, learning style and motivation in early childhood will transfer to the elementary classroom. Curious, open to new ideas, able to initiate projects, focus, and persist at them, attentive to teacher, able to put new learning to use through reflection and interpretation.

IV. Language Development
The ability to interact and communicate effectively with adults and peers is essential for success in the elementary classroom. Uses language socially to express feelings, get needs met, get information, has strong vocabulary and concept development (spatial and temporal relationships, sequence, causality, and meanings of words), frame questions, recognize and use rhyming and word play, sing songs, tells and/or plays out stories. Notices print in the environment, understands story structure, sequence, cause and effect, and writes/recognizes some letters.

V. Cognition and General Knowledge
Children who have been encouraged to explore, experience and question the world around them through play are ready for the more structured learning experiences of elementary school when they understand the physical properties of objects around them, understand relationships between objects such as comparisons, measurement, mathematical operations and problem-solving, and understand cultural conventions.

Of course every classroom will include children across the developmental continuum, so it would be surprising if all the children aligned with all the standards. But as the teacher sees the balance of the class coming into alignment, she can increase the amount of time she leads with her lessons rather than following the children's lead and responding. Throughout the year in a classroom with 4s, 5s and even young 6s, the teacher will move nimbly between guiding play and offering direct instruction, but as the children's brains and bodies mature the trend will always be moving towards a greater interest and capacity in hearing what the teacher has to say. Still, play continues to be an important mode of learning throughout the primary years.

How Play Builds Foundations for Academic Learning

The single most important attitude a child can have for academic learning is the belief that "I can do it!" A child who sees herself as "too little," or as someone who cannot do what is requested of her, or as someone unable to succeed in school, starts with a real deficit. A quality play experience is designed to give each child a solid academic, social, and emotional foundation for future academic learning by helping him learn to manage his behavior and recognize his good contributions to a group while also meeting his own needs. This is a child who will be able to succeed in an elementary school classroom environment.

In self-initiated play, the child controls the situation and sets the limits. Children will try harder to achieve a goal they set themselves, and persistence is one of the character traits that contributes to success. Children cannot "fail" in play; they either succeed at what they are trying to play, or they change the game to one that is achievable because their goal is to keep the game going. In this process they learn to negotiate, contribute new ideas, think flexibly and compromise. Children are more willing to take risks and try new ideas while playing than when they are directed to do something a certain way. The creativity and confidence built through self-initiated play will serve them well once they reach the more conforming environment they will encounter in first grade.

Along with the academics that children are learning through their play, children are also developing socially and emotionally. They are learning how to get along with each other, how to understand themselves, and how to manage their feelings and to be part of a group. Finally, in a busy play environment, children learn to focus and concentrate on their own interests and not to be distracted by what others are doing nearby. All of these skills are also very important for Kindergarten readiness. It defies adult logic, but play really does teach a child the skills he needs to succeed academically.

The Teacher is Crucial to Play

Besides providing the time and space for children to interact and try out their ideas, the teacher observes how well each child is playing. Is the child engaged in an activity? Is she using language? Is she comfortable playing near or with other children? Do you see signs of concentration, problem-solving, or persistence? If so, you are watching a child construct knowledge about how the world works: how the pieces fit into a puzzle; which blocks will balance and which will fall; how other children respond to her attempts to make friends; and how to recover when a first attempt at any of these fails to get the desired response.

Some children need help developing their play so it can constructively guide their learning. It is not uncommon for a child to be distracted by the desire to be in relationships with other children, and instead of playing this child may interrupt or bother the other children or the teacher. Other children need help to figure out how to initiate an activity or how to get along with others without being the center of the play; playing with a friend is different from playing alone or with an adult. Children who are not experiencing success in play will have difficulty enjoying their learning experience in elementary school.

Teachers can facilitate the social and emotional learning in the play by giving children friendly words to say to enter into someone else's game. Sometimes a teacher may need to plan ways to encourage children with the same interests to "find" each other and begin an activity together. The teacher also builds self-initiation and resilience in individual children by piquing their curiosity and helping them focus on what really interests them.

It is always tempting for the busy teacher to think that while the children are playing she can sit at her desk and catch up on paperwork, but she is a crucial component to the play. The dollhouse needs the teacher tuned in to play just as much as it needs a sink, stove, dishes in the cupboard and dolls in a bed. The block area needs the teacher tuned in to the play just as much as it needs blocks, vehicles and little people. The teacher's small passing comments provide invaluable input for children at just the moments that they can use them. We will delve into this more deeply in subsequent chapters.

Academic Skills as Seen in Play

Play is full of joy and creativity, which build fluid thinking; it will help children understand the more abstract ideas they will learn in elementary school. The play curriculum in the 4s, 5s and 6s is infused with academics taught within the child's play. As the child plays, ample opportunities to succeed in individual and group problem-solving tasks arise. These tasks may be cognitive, motor, or social; success in any of these areas leads to an enhanced self-concept, self-confidence, and the ability to self-actualize. A child who feels good about himself, who has been encouraged to be curious about the world, and who has experienced success in a group learning environment will be ready and eager to learn.

Children are building learning foundations in every area of the play-based classroom, as follows.

Pre-Reading Skills

LISTENING

The ability to sit quietly and listen to a story, or to let another child speak, knowing that each child will have an opportunity, is essential to classroom success. Story time, group time, and music are frequent so children can practice these skills. In play, when a teacher helps children really *listen* to each other as they work out a problem or conflict, children can practice listening in a real-life situation.

ORAL LANGUAGE

Children must be able to express ideas and abstract concepts such as feelings. Dramatic play provides constant opportunities to negotiate, explain, plan, and take roles, which all require the child to develop the reciprocity and abstraction of oral language. Hearing the patterns of language aids in both grammar and sentence structure. Vocabulary is learned when the teacher listens in to their conversations and provides words for relevant things, ideas, and feelings.

COMPREHENSION

As children act out scenes during block play or dramatic play, they clarify their world view, which leads to better comprehension of both fictional and factual information. Like the stories in a book, their dramatic play also has different characters, a setting, and a plot as the action moves forward. Thus they are experiencing story structure, which will later aid them in understanding the stories they are learning to read.

VISUAL DISCRIMINATION

Reading requires that children be able to notice small details, such as the difference between "a" and "o." Assembling a puzzle and playing matching games develop this skill, as do scientific observations where the teacher directs children to notice details of the objects under study.

SEQUENCING OF EVENTS

Stories each have a beginning, middle, and end; children must understand this logical sequence. Common routines (such as dinner: cook the food, set the table, call the family, eat, clear the table, wash the dishes) are natural sequences that are always done in the same order. Classroom routines and dramatic play support this sense of order. Children who are encouraged to "read" familiar books by telling stories from the pictures are also practicing sequencing.

UNDERSTANDING AND USING SYMBOLS

Play is also where children develop the concept of symbols. Using a block to symbolize a chimney or a stick to symbolize a magic wand is the same skill that will eventually lead to understanding that the letters "C-A-T" symbolize a small furry animal that says "meow." Understanding that one object can stand for another is the root of both imaginative play and of reading.

Prewriting Skills

FINE MOTOR SKILLS

Dressing dolls, buttoning, opening and closing containers, and manipulating Legos, puzzle pieces, and blocks are some of the many ways these skills are built into the play curriculum. The art or writing center will have a variety of thick and thin pencils and crayons, small and large paintbrushes, rulers, hole-punchers, scissors and many ways to exercise the small muscles of children's hands which need to develop strength, coordination and stamina for handwriting.

HAND–EYE COORDINATION

Brain pathways that connect what the eye sees with what the hand does are built through practice and repetition. They are developing hand–eye coordination through large motor activities such as climbing as well as the tasks that build fine motor skills. With experience, children's craft creations are often very complex and call for great dexterity.

LETTER KNOWLEDGE

Four- and 5-year-olds are beginning to take an active interest in letters and numerals. Writing begins with drawings that tell a story ("This is my mom. She's cooking dinner.") As the PreK year progresses, their drawings become more detailed and they begin to include letters from a nearby alphabet chart. A card file near the art center with some high-interest sight words (friends' names, "mom," "dog," etc.) will enhance their art and become part of their play. By the end of the year they may be writing notes to their friends, or labeling their building projects. Teachers can encourage this by taking dictation or helping them spell words they want to use.

PRE-MATH SKILLS

Although very young children can recite numbers in order, it takes years of experience with objects to develop the concepts that support mathematical thinking. You will notice the recurrence of blocks and other manipulative objects as a prime tool for learning the following concepts which form the foundations for math.

ONE-TO-ONE CORRESPONDENCE

The ability to match one object with one number as it is counted comes after many experiences matching sets where there is only one corresponding "partner," such as putting 18 pegs into 18 holes on a pegboard. Setting the table, real or pretend, supports this learning with one plate for each person, one fork for each plate, etc.

ORDERING

Arranging things from smaller to larger is something children spontaneously do when they are putting together nesting boxes or organize their blocks. As they begin to learn the numerals they will practice putting them in order as part of their play.

COUNTING

The ability to count objects correctly comes after children have mastered one-to-one correspondence and ordering. The teacher leads counting activities at circle time, which the children carry into their self-initiated activities.

EQUIVALENCE

By understanding that two separate quantities can be equal (that is, two short blocks stacked on top of each other are the same height as one tall block), children understand that $2 + 2 = 4$. Small unit blocks are designed to demonstrate equivalence: two small squares are the same size as one "unit" rectangle, etc. Friends may also experiment with balance scales or count things to see if each has the same amount.

GROUPING BY SIMILARITY

Sorting objects based on a common trait, such as color, shape, or size, leads to understanding set theory in math and classification in science. Children group and put like objects together as they clean up from activities as well as in play. Having shadow shapes on the block shelf is one way to encourage both matching and grouping.

SHAPE RECOGNITION, SIZE RELATIONSHIPS, AND SPATIAL RELATIONSHIPS

The various shapes and sizes in the unit blocks are a wonderful resource for developing math vocabulary. When the children finish a building and want to show it to the teacher, that is a springboard for modeling words like "bigger," "wider," "taller," "next to," "above," "far," "round," "pointy," "cylindrical," and many more! Children effortlessly pick up words the teacher uses in connection with their activities.

PROBLEM-SOLVING

Children often set problems for themselves as they play. How will we decide who can be the "mom"? How can I make this building stay up? Why won't these puzzle pieces fit together? These repeated experiences of inventing successful solutions makes a child confident that he can deal with the small and large problems of life.

DIVERGENT THINKING AND PERSISTENCE

The first attempt at solving a problem may not work. In play children will learn to be flexible and try a variety of approaches and strategies on a problem when the first one fails to solve it. Trial and error in any given area leads to more abstract strategies as the child matures; success leads to persistence, because the child is confident that she will be able to succeed eventually.

Explaining Learning in Play to Parents and Colleagues

Posting signs with information about the learning that goes on in various play areas around the room can give parents and colleagues insight to what the children are learning through their play. For example, a sign over the dramatic play area might say:

In the Play House Children Learn:

- To talk to each other
- To listen to each other
- To see through another person's eyes
- Small motor skills—dressing dolls or selves
- To develop ideas, characters and plot
- One-to-one correspondence setting the table
- About order when putting toys away.

Figure 1.4 Multiple learning foundations are developed in dramatic play
Source: Photo courtesy of Monaire Taylor.

Lists for signs like this for other areas of the classroom are located in Appendix 2.

If a parent is volunteering in your classroom, the job assignment can also be structured to help the parent learn about the way that the children are learning these background skills in play: "Mrs. Jimenez, while you are watching the dollhouse will you please watch for opportunities to encourage the children to speak to each other about their ideas? Like if Sandy is putting a doll in the stroller you can ask her to tell the others where she is getting ready to go, or if you see two children who want the same toy you can help each of them tell the other what they

(1) Once the children know the routine they can choose and play with little or no teacher guidance. A child independently decides to paint a picture. She follows the learned routine and begins by getting her apron on and pulling up her sleeves.

(2) Next she gets a piece of easel paper from the shelf and puts it on the easel with the magnets. The colors bring a sensuous pleasure as she begins to paint, color after color as the painting evolves. She develops hand–eye coordination, small muscle control, and a visual sense of balance and symmetry.

(3) Without needing to make "something" she is guided by her own self-expression to paint and explore her inner world, strengthening her self-knowledge and sense of self-worth. Full body movements strengthen coordination of left and right sides of the brain thus building pre-reading skills, tracking, ordering, sequencing, and motor planning.

(4) She writes her name on the picture and hangs it on the drying rack, takes off her apron and washes her hands. Routine complete, she is off to choose anew. Knowing routines gives children freedom to choose. She learns to make her choices and their consequences with freedom and confidence, taking care of herself in the big busy world of school.

Figure 1.5 Skills learned while painting
Source: Photos courtesy of Monaire Taylor.

want and see if they can make a plan together." In this way you are both helping the children grow their skills and expand their play, and helping the parent understand the value of the play and your intention behind the activities you offer the children. Chapter 5 offers a number of tips for facilitating language in your classroom, and these can be helpful to parent volunteers as well.

Another tool the teacher can use to explain learning is classroom documentation. Photos of an activity are the most common basis for documentation, with captions added to explain how that activity contributes to the children's growth and learning. Pictures drawn by children about a class experience, captioned with their own words (written by the child or dictated to an adult, as appropriate) to describe what captured their interest, also offer insightful documentation although not so much about the teacher's goals. Documentation may be about a concept rather than an event, such as "Ways we show kindness in our classroom," with each child contributing a drawing and description of a kindness they showed to a classmate. Documentation can take the form of a simple booklet printed out, stapled together and put on the bookshelf, or a poster board on the wall. Whatever form it takes, it gives the teacher another opportunity to explain the foundations she is helping the children build. The children will enjoy recalling the activity both for themselves and to tell their parents about the experience. But with the teacher's insights, the parents learn that the day when the children made oobleck was also the day that the children had a lesson in measuring, waiting for a turn, acknowledging peer requests and passing materials to others (saying "please pass" and "thank you," of course!), and studying the different properties of dry cornstarch and wet cornstarch.

Notes

1. Gopnik, Alison, A. Meltzoff, and P. Kuhl, *The Scientist in the Crib: Minds, Brains, and How Children Learn*, New York: William Morrow and Co., 1999.
2. Miller, Edward, and Joan Almon, *Crisis in the Kindergarten: Why Children Need to Play in School*, College Park, MD: Alliance for Childhood, 2009.
3. Goleman, Daniel, *Emotional Intelligence*, New York: Bantam Books, 1995.
4. Schweinhart, Lawrence, J. Montie, A. Xiang, W.S. Barnett, C. Belfield, and M. Nores, *Lifetime Effects: The HighScope Perry Preschool Study through Age 40* (Monographs of the HighScope Educational Research Foundation, 14), Ypsilanti, MI: HighScope Press, 2005.
5. Schweinhart, Lawrence, and D.P. Weikart, *Lasting Differences: The HighScope Preschool Curriculum Comparison Study through Age 23* (Monographs of the HighScope Educational Research Foundation, 12), Ypsilanti, MI: HighScope Press, 1997.
6. Farran, Dale, *Federal Preschool Development Grants: Evaluation Needed*, Washington, DC: Brookings Institute, 2016.
7. Moffitt, Terrie, L. Arseneault, D. Belsky, N. Dickson, R. Hancox, H. Harrington, R. Houts, R. Poulton, B. Roberts, S. Ross, M. Sears, W.M. Thomson, and A. Caspi, "A gradient of childhood self-control predicts health, wealth and public safety," *Proceedings of the National Academy of Science*, February 15, 2011, Vol. 108, No. 7.
8. Cited in Miller, Edward, and Joan Almon, *Crisis in the Kindergarten: Why Children Need to Play in School*, College Park, MD: Alliance for Childhood, 2009.

Chapter 2

The 3R Framework
Room, Routines, and Relationships

Key Information in this Chapter
- Step-by-step planning for a year of learning
- How to set up a classroom that supports your teaching goals
- Establishing the routines that will support the flow of daily life in your classroom
- Building intentional relationships with children, parents, and classroom helpers

As we saw in Chapter 1, young children are active learners who need to integrate their increasingly complex brains with the rest of their development. In a sense, they "learn with their bodies" and "think through their play." Fine and gross motor activities not only make them more skillful physically, but also stimulate the brain centers that control these functions. Speaking, listening, solving problems, practicing self-control, and socializing with their peers also stimulate growth in different parts of the brain. One task of the brains of 4s and 5s is to integrate the brain and body into one well-functioning machine by the sixth birthday. The most efficient way to accomplish this is through guided play, which is different from what we think of as "free play."

When children are playing, their brains are constantly multi-tasking: listening to their friends, explaining their own ideas, watching and imitating others, manipulating their environment, and learning to control their strong feelings when problems arise. Children need a helper and guide to enable them to negotiate this maze of actions, thoughts, and feelings successfully. That is why the play is supervised by adults who understand the child's development and experience, and who have the skills to help them understand how the world works. Statements like:

- "Your friend doesn't understand what you want when your voice is so loud. Can you use a friendlier voice to tell her what you want?"
- "When tall block towers fall down people can get hurt."
- "We put puzzles on the shelf when we're done so that other children know that it is their turn to use them."

are guideposts along the way that the teacher provides in the moment they are needed.

In any given classroom there will be a wide range of maturity—even among children of the same age. Young 4-year-olds who have never been to preschool may function at a 3- or 3½-level at first, but—because they are 4, not 3—they will progress faster than a 3-year-old would. Likewise, a mature 5-year-old may function at a 6-year-old level in some areas, but as a much younger child in other areas, depending on her experience. Children with older siblings may appear to be more mature than they actually are, as they mimic some of the behaviors they see at home. Similarly, children with younger siblings may have retained less mature behaviors as they see those behaviors working for their younger brothers and sisters. In addition, the temperament of each child may challenge him in different situations and require extra support. The slow-to-warm-up child will need a little time to watch others before being asked to say her name in circle, whereas the outgoing child may need to be reminded to let others speak.

All this can be summarized in one sentence: *The teacher will need to differentiate her instruction to meet the varying developmental levels of the children.* Development builds on itself, as the brain and the body mature. Trying to skip a developmental stage so that the whole class can be at the same level may be tempting for the busy teacher, but in the long run, learning will be faster and easier if each child is working in his own "zone of proximal development" (starting with what they can already do and adding one new thing). In a classroom with combined grades this spread will be even broader, and the teaching will thus be more creative and flexible.

The most effective way to do this is to offer a range of activities and let the children find their own level of proximal development. The miracle of child development is that healthy children are *most* interested in trying something that offers just the right amount of challenge. Activities that are too easy will quickly lose their appeal. Activities that are too difficult will soon be left unfinished, as the child goes in search of an activity that offers a challenge that she is able to master. As the children learn and grow, the play activities planned by the teacher will become more complex, to provide new challenges as the children are ready for them.

There is a place in the PreK classroom for direct instruction by the teacher: pre-literacy and math skills, hearing stories that broaden their understanding of themselves and the world, and enjoying shared experiences that will develop a sense of community. A well-rounded program will include these experiences, as well as the opportunity to explore their interests and hone their skills through guided play. This chapter introduces the "nuts and bolts" of setting up the play areas and tips on guiding the play. Future chapters will go more deeply into the topic of play, and will also suggest techniques for teaching academic skills as well.

The Room

Setting up the Classroom for Active Learning

Clear and organized play spaces are the first step to constructive learning through play. The areas should be well defined and contained so children do not inadvertently walk through and disrupt other children's play. As you set up each area, address all of these questions:

- What kind of play would I like to see here?
- Have I selected the right toys to suggest appropriate play to the children?
- How many children can successfully play here at one time?
- Is there enough space and materials for everyone?
- Are the materials easy for the children to take out and put away?

Environment and Traffic Patterns

A good set-up is often referred to as "the other teacher in the room" because a well-organized classroom can help you nearly as much as having an assistant! The classroom should support your supervision and teaching. Think carefully about how the children are using the play areas you set up and how they move around the classroom. Is there enough room for the number of children who will be playing there? Think about the traffic patterns and the walkways. Can the walkway around the table still be used when the children are sitting at the table and the chairs are pulled out? Book areas need to be in a quiet space and feel cozy. Blocks need room. Messy art projects should be near a place to wash hands and a drying rack or a place to put the art to dry. Sending children across the classroom to wash their hands after finger painting is a set-up for trouble.

As you look at each area, think through how it will reinforce the routine that supports this kind of play in the space. Are the aprons near the easel? Will the highly social areas such as dollhouse, art or blocks distract children working quietly nearby? A quiet corner, somewhat isolated, is ideal for books or puzzles that require concentration and focus. Think twice before you place art materials near books as creative, inexperienced children may think that books are suitable for scissors and crayons. Place materials on low shelves near the tables or rugs on which they will be used. Legos and toys with lots of pieces are great on a rug but need a bin to contain them when they are not in active use. Be sure the shelves are well organized and uncluttered so it is easy for children to find the materials they need, and also easy to put them away. Putting activities with many pieces on a small tray or in a box lid will help children to keep all the pieces together, so the toy will be appealing to the next child. Look at all the variables as you work to build a healthy, constructive play experience for the children.

A well-planned play area will help the children manage their own materials without getting in each other's way. For example, if you are setting out baby doll washing, think about what the children would like: soap and a washcloth, maybe a brush and small bottles of colored water for medicine or pretend lotion. If you want the space to send the message that the activity is for two children, set it up with two tubs each containing a doll and matching sets of equipment, each on a bath towel, with an apron on each of two chairs. When your set-up is clear it helps the children know whether or not there is room; you can remind them they can have a turn later if both chairs are occupied: "Come back when a chair is empty; it looks like Andy will be done soon and there will be room. Andy, will you tell Cael when you are done?" At the beginning of the year, before the children have learned to share and cooperate, these very explicit arrangements will help children to play near others without conflict. As the year progresses and children grow into a more cooperative stage of development these areas may become more communal in nature.

Defined Spaces

The classroom should be divided into areas that clearly tell the children what to do as they play in each area. Ideally, each classroom should have a:

- block plus trains and/or small vehicle area
- manipulative and puzzle area
- art and drawing area (which will evolve into a writing center as children are ready)
- library with soft rugs or pillow and a stuffed animal or two
- dollhouse area with a space for cooking and eating, and a place for baby dolls to sleep
- science area with real objects from nature to manipulate, and related non-fiction picture books
- sensory play area for water play, sand, playdough, or other sensory activities.

Designate spaces with room dividers or furniture, such as a low shelf, which still allow the teacher to see the entire room. Area rugs or tables and chairs can also designate a space. For table activities, the children can see how many may play there at one time by the number of chairs placed at the table. Some activities work well for children who are standing, such as playing at a sensory table; put tape on the floor, or use the number of aprons to define how many may use that space as well. These rules keep areas from getting too crowded to enjoy.

In an area like the playhouse where the furniture may create the play area, it is especially important to put out just enough play materials. Too many pieces will distract the children from purposeful play. If the children in the dollhouse are young and inexperienced, a kitchen table in the playhouse that seats four needs only four plates, four teacups and four saucers in the cupboard. The dress-up toys that work best are generic: jackets, aprons, scarves, purses, shoes and hats (be sure to include boys' clothing). With blankets and bedding, and some cooking pots and utensils, this is quite a lot of equipment in one play area. As the children get older and more imaginative in their play you may want to increase the number of props—adding a birthday cake or a pizza to the refrigerator to stimulate play, or bringing in small dishes and a bottle and high chair for the baby doll. Generally 4- and 5-year-olds do not need plastic food, as they are old enough to serve and eat "pretend food" which can be whatever they want it to be. There is a difference between a plastic birthday cake, which can launch a play theme, and a lump of plastic peas which does not. The teacher may keep add-in toys in a nearby cupboard, such as community helper costumes, a doctor's bag, or a cash register, and only bring them out when the play suggests that they are needed. A cardboard box decorated by the children with wheels and doors parked by the kitchen adds another dimension to the play; now children can go shopping, to the doctor, or whatever the imagination desires.

In a space like the block area, shelves usually create the boundary on the edge of a rug area; this also helps keep the noise of block play down. A rug in the blocks should have a very flat pile so the children's blocks won't tip over when they build. Accessories like people, animals, cars and trucks can be set in low baskets or stood up on the shelves to help the children see the toys and choose, thus building their ideas and extending their play. The teacher's goal in displaying materials is to draw the children to the activity so they will engage in constructive play.

Areas that Invite Children to Play

Children will be most intrigued by a set-up that reflects the things the children see around them in their daily lives, or that they are curious about. The play you set up should have meaning for the children and help them understand the world around them. It will help them understand their relationships with others as they play different roles. If you know a child in your group has a baby at home who is learning to crawl and getting into the older child's things, you can help the older child by setting up the baby dolls with a big brother or sister doll who has interesting things to play with. Soon you will find the frustrated big brothers and sisters very interested in your set-up, talking about controlling the baby (who is as uncontrollable as all babies are). An outlet like this drains frustrated energy and the annoyances of trying to be a good big sibling into play rather than directing it towards the real baby—a win–win for the entire family. At holiday time, gluing with sparkly things similar to those that children aren't allowed to touch at home is an alluring activity. Making or recycling wrapping paper, and wrapping up boxes or other things can also have appeal.

36   The 3R Framework

Figure 2.1 Clear and inviting choices of manipulative toys
Source: Photo courtesy of Monaire Taylor.

Place toys together so they suggest doing something constructive or thoughtful. Trucks, people the right size to ride in them, street signs, and wooden trees and blocks for the trucks to carry, can all be lined up together on the shelf. This suggests how to play constructively with the trucks. When teachers set up tempting invitations to play, they subtly draw the children in and suggest ideas that the child can frame and enhance with his own repertoire of experiences. In this way the teacher creates opportunities for the child to expand his play, attention span, imagination, and confidence as he succeeds in the play. If children seem bored, or are wandering around, look critically at the set-up and think about how to create stronger invitations to play that suggest interesting ideas—and make them more complicated as children get older and become more sophisticated players. Your goal is to make it nearly impossible for the children to walk past without being drawn in.

Combinations of toys and how they are displayed are important factors. A pile of toys in a box looks like nothing but a pile of stuff. Separate them and put them on a shelf and suddenly the children have ideas for playing with them. A water table with boats and little people who fit on the boats and little plastic fish makes sense and gives ideas for play; a water table with sail boats and baby dolls the same size and magnetized fish in the water table does not clearly suggest an activity to the children. The teacher wants the children to be learning through play. If the children get silly because they aren't clear about how to use materials, it will not generate constructive ideas or lead to play that is sustaining. On the other hand, baby dolls with tiny boats (boats that could be the baby's *toys*) and other bathing equipment would work fine, because once again there is a cohesive theme of "baby in the bath."

Children with little experience and imagination will need set-ups that offer stronger suggestions for play. For example, for a child who does not seem to know how to use play materials, you can set up very specific toys on a special tray for her, such as little props to play out the story of a favorite picture book. Place them on a small table with the book to see if that will spark her imagination; it may also spark an interest in looking at books!

Growing through the Year

In the beginning of the school year when the children are younger, the toys and equipment should be set up in a clear simple way to match the children's interests and abilities. Especially at this time, when the children are establishing new relationships with the teacher, she wants the children to succeed with every activity and to feel that they can do everything. The puzzles will be easy. The art materials will begin with just blank paper, crayons and scissors; as the children grow more skillful, glue, markers, colored paper, and watercolor paints will be gradually added. The block area will begin with just blocks with trains or cars; other props, such as people, signs, and animals can be added later. As the year progresses the classroom challenges should grow. Teachers will have more success with the children's learning if they start the year showing the children that they can do it all, and that this learning is fun and easy!

Figure 2.2 The block shelf early in the year
Source: Photo courtesy of Monaire Taylor.

Figure 2.3 The enhanced block shelf later in the year
Source: Photo courtesy of Monaire Taylor.

Keeping the Play Areas Fresh

Entering the classroom should feel to the child a little like you feel when you wander through a favorite store. Each discrete play area, and the room as a whole, should look pleasant and welcoming and attractive to the children. The teacher needs to change toys and add appealing props to re-stimulate play in each area when the toys that have been there are losing their attraction. A basket of zoo animals will extend block play by suggesting a new theme, just as new colors at the painting easel suggest another kind of painting, or strollers in the playhouse draw another level of interest to this play. A vase of flowers at the manipulative table will draw some children to play there. The areas remain the same but additional toys are brought in to stimulate and extend the play over the course of the year. Teachers need to observe carefully so that they can see when to leave a set-up intact for a little longer because the children are particularly interested in it, and when the set-up is not working well and ought to be changed to draw the children in. Some activities will be interesting for a long time, while others will be "played out" in a shorter period of time. Playdough is always popular, whereas water colors are especially interesting and nice on a rainy day. Don't hesitate to try the same thing several times over the course of several months; as the children get older and more able, ideas that didn't appeal before may come into favor.

Choosing Toys

Children should have opportunities to play with toys made of a variety of materials: plastic, wood, metal and cloth. Toys should be age appropriate; this means the toy has meaning for the child as well as being a toy that children can manage on their own without adult help.

Choose toys that inspire creativity and imagination and teach pro-social values. You want toys that elicit the social and emotional skills you are teaching so that the children can practice them over and over in their play. When you are actively helping children remember to talk instead of hitting, you may not want to put action figures, dinosaurs, or other aggressive animal figures out. Books, movies, and TV shows about action heroes may also stimulate aggressive play, so avoid putting these "branded" items in your room. Be alert to toys that are designed to entertain children rather than stimulate their imaginations. Battery-operated toys, for example, are fun to watch—and that's what the children do—they watch them rather than engage with them and use their own ideas to play out the things that are important to them. In the same way, children who watch a popular movie may want to simply replay it over and over, demanding that everyone in the game stick to their role and lines from the movie—which is helpful to try to understand the movie, but not so helpful in trying to understand their own lives. If the teacher feels that children have gotten stuck in this type of repetitive play she can ask them to discuss and agree upon their plan before they begin.

AGE-APPROPRIATE PLAY ACTIVITIES

Activities in the "Interactive Interest Centers" chart below are appropriate for children at the ages of 4 and 5. Teach children to follow the procedure for the materials and equipment before allowing them to use the area. Start the year as simply as possible while keeping it interesting, then add supplies to the shelf as the children's thinking gets more complex and play skills increase. For example, drawing with chalk, markers or oil pastels is not very different from drawing with a crayon, but it does add variety and use hand muscles differently, and could attract children who think crayons are boring to the drawing table to practice writing and drawing. In the beginning a minimum of supplies keeps clean-up time manageable and focuses the children on proper use and care. String, collage, or stamp pads and stamps all come later as the children develop their abilities to manage all the supplies. At the start of the year the children need to succeed and feel supported more than they need a lot of stimulation, because the new setting and children provide plenty of stimulation. By the end of the year the teacher may have put every supply she has on the art shelf for creative children to choose from, because they can now use them all independently and constructively.

Some teachers make up small sets of toys that suggest a play idea and keep them on hand to help a child who needs extra support. These are small toys to use on a

Figure 2.4 A small set—micromachines, pebbles, tube, wood bits
Source: Photo courtesy of Monaire Taylor.

table top with a theme that encourages language development. It is helpful for the children to have sets that relate to their experiences, like a barber shop or a zoo or the doctor's office. Playmobil® makes a lot of these sets or you can find odds and ends to make your own. Some popular themes you can put together are: Garage, School, House, Camping, Zoo, Gardening, Wildlife adventures, Airport, Store, Picnic, Bike ride, Doctor/Hospital. Small cars, with empty paper towel and toilet paper rolls and a few wide tongue depressors presented in a box lid to help the child keep the cars on the table, can be a set. Two-inch dolls with diapers and cribs and a blanket, and maybe a tiny bottle, can be a set that is quite comforting for a child missing his mommy. A small handful of baseball or soccer players, with a field marked on green construction paper, is a popular set.

Limit the use of sets so they will be novel and interesting when you need them; save them for a rainy day when the children need to be inside all day, or use them to pair children who will learn from each other's ideas or social skills. Save them as a treat for a rejected child, as the set may draw a new friend to play. These toys are your tools to create the learning situations you see that your children need to move forward in their growth.

Interactive Interest Centers throughout the Year

As the year progresses, the teacher will add and subtract toys to each area as she sees the need to extend play, or sees items no longer being used well. It is just as important to remove unused toys and keep down clutter as it is to add toys. In a classroom of young 4-year-olds, the basic materials in each area will be sufficient at the beginning of the year, and may not need much augmentation for several months as the children are more focused on learning about each other and the classroom than about the toys. On the other hand, the classroom might need more materials in place at the beginning of the year in a 5-year-old classroom with children who spent the past year in a play-based preschool.

Table 2.1 gives examples of how various centers may flex during the course of the year.

Planning for an Outdoor Classroom

Outdoor play is not an optional activity for 4- and 5-year-olds, but a part of your curriculum. It is not a "recess," because young children continue to need adult help with their physical development. Children need to move so their growing bodies will receive pumping, oxygenated blood. Vigorous and varied outdoor play builds the spatial awareness and motor planning that are foundations for academic success as well as strong bodies. Creative teachers who work where there is limited time allotted for physical education or recess often re-label it so they can accommodate the needs of their students, including something like Perceptual Motor time in their schedules along with PE and recess. Coordination, strength and stamina all are part of developing:

- eye dominance to learn to read
- ability to transfer information from the board at the front of the class to their paper on the table
- the small muscle coordination needed to learn to write
- the balance and trunk strength that allows children to stay upright in their chairs or sit quietly on the rug.

The "outdoor classroom" in a PreK or Kindergarten program can offer as wide a variety of learning experiences as the indoors. The ideal classroom for 4- and 5-year-old children has an attached bathroom, a sink for art clean-up, and an adjacent play area right outside the classroom, but as early childhood programs expand they are often given imperfect spaces that require the teacher's most inventive thinking to accommodate the children's needs. The resourceful teacher can enrich any outdoor space to provide an outdoor learning environment for the children—though she may need a cart to haul her equipment back and forth onto the playground, or need to appeal to the school leadership to adapt the outdoor space for the use of her class. As in the indoor classroom, the teacher's presence and intentional set-up and plan for the children's activities will result in more learning. The environment should be rich enough that if some children choose to play outdoors most of the time, they will get the same opportunities for learning that they would inside. The structure and accountability for managing one's own behavior is just as important outside as it is inside. Routines and procedures should be created for the children's safety, to increase the children's enjoyment, and to support the teacher's goals.

Table 2.1 Basic furnishings in each center, and how to extend them through the year

Type of Center, Space, and Equipment	Skills that are Practiced	Start of Year Basic Materials	Add-in Materials for Older Children
Blocks and Trains Large flat rug, low shelves on two sides, next to a wall or corner to protect block play from pathways.	Gross motor and fine motor skills, math concepts (size, shapes, position words, sorting, ordering, counting, measuring), cooperation and negotiation, language, creativity.	Wooden unit blocks. Trains with tracks; cars, small animals, and people each in their own basket. Small set of large hollow wooden building blocks.	Other sizes, colors, and/or shapes of blocks, traffic signs, paper and pencil for making signs, masking tape for marking roads on the floor or taping up signs, dollhouse people, vehicles and furniture, fabric squares, a basket of dishes for dramatic play. Rotate materials as new ideas are needed.
Dramatic Play House Size varies with the age of the children. Five-year-olds can play in larger groups, so need more space. Younger children need room for 3 or 4. Works well next to the block area, or another space for extended dramatic play, such as a store or restaurant.	Language, cooperation, social skills, fine motor skills (dressing dolls, unscrewing caps), emotional self-regulation, imagination.	Child-sized furniture: small table and chairs, sink, stove, refrigerator; baby dolls, small blankets and doll clothes; basic dress-up clothes (aprons, vests, hats, purses, lunch box); play dishes (set of 4) with plates, cups, cooking pot, frying pan, tea kettle, utensils.	Full-length mirror, doll beds or high chair, more variety of dress-up clothes (skirts, jewelry, jackets, a white doctor's coat, coveralls), first-aid kit, tool box and hard hat, etc. *Tip: keep some items out of sight, but handy to get when needed.*
Math/Cognitive Toys and Small Puzzles Tables and chairs near low shelves that hold the materials. Trays are helpful to organize but not required.	Fine motor skills, problem-solving strategies, number concepts, patterns, persistence, numbers and letters (ABC and numeral puzzles).	Small puzzles of varying difficulty (15–25 pieces), nesting cups, beads to string, Legos (*larger pieces for younger children, smaller pieces for older children*), shape sorters.	More Legos, Lincoln Logs, counting toys or small people, small building materials, peg board and pegs, mix 'n' match games, sorting trays with buttons or other small items, puzzles with more pieces (25–50), floor puzzles.
Art Area Best near the sink! Easels, drying rack or line, large easy-clean table and chairs, trays, containers for materials, storage shelves or drawers for a variety of art supplies.	Self-expression, creativity, fine motor skills, names of colors, shapes and textures, self-regulation, symbolic thinking, eye-hand coordination, self-esteem.	Tempura paints, cups and brushes, aprons, a variety of paper colors and sizes, glue sticks or small glue bottles, scissors, crayons, list of children's names (or laminated name cards).	Markers, colored pencils, collage materials (cloth, beads, beans, items from nature), water colors and small brushes, stencils, hole-punchers, yarn, painter's tape, rulers, recycled materials for 3-D art.

Area	Skills	Materials	Notes
Science Area Table, fish tank, terrarium, bug boxes, or cage for classroom pet, if desired. If there is a suitable outdoor area, add a garden.	Observation skills, five senses, fine motor skills, curiosity, knowledge of the world, vocabulary, pre-literacy.	Magnifiers, items from nature to study, colored plastic pieces to look through, prisms, magnets, science books with pictures, printed labels for each exhibit.	Balance scale, egg (hourglass) timers, silkworms or other small creatures to study, feel box with items to describe, small bottles with different scents (whole spices), brooms, rakes, watering cans, natural collections (pine cones, leaves, seeds, etc.), notebooks to record what they see (older children).
Sensory Motor Area Water or sand table, or plastic tubs with tight lids to store other sensory materials, aprons, table and chairs.	Emotional self-regulation, imagination, fine motor skills, language.	Sand, water, beans, or cornmeal with containers for pouring and measuring; or (at a table) playdough or wet clay, and kitchen implements.	For other materials and accessories, please refer to the sensory section in Chapter 5.
Quiet Area/Library Book display rack or baskets for books, rug, comfortable seating (rockers, pillows, or couch).	Emotional self-regulation, pre-literacy skills, language and imagination.	Minimum of eight to ten picture books on the shelf or display, one science book relating to what is in the science area, one chapter book with only a few small pictures, one book about cars and trucks or machines and construction, reference books (body parts, insects, birds, space, etc.), poetry anthology.	Felt board and book character pieces, or a small table with a display of props for retelling a familiar story (along with the book), books children have written and illustrated, magazines, stuffed animals to read to, glasses frames ("reading glasses"). By end of year, 20–30 books.
Listening/Music Center (optional) Small table and chairs, CD player with earphones.	Listening skills, pre-literacy, music appreciation, emotional self-regulation.	Story CDs with matching books, CDs of instrumental or choral music. Teach children how to use the CD player without teacher assistance.	If you have the right acoustics, add some simple musical instruments, such as a xylophone, small bells with different tones, drums, or rhythm instruments (or these may go outside on a porch).

Figure 2.5 Vigorous play develops the body that supports the mind
Source: Photo courtesy of Monaire Taylor.

Figure 2.6 Scientific observation requires only simple equipment
Source: Photo courtesy of Spencer Perry.

In addition to all the skills that are learned inside the classroom, the outdoor classroom provides an opportunity to work on some additional skills that are difficult to do indoors: gross motor activities (climbing, skipping, jumping rope), noisier activities (carpentry, playing musical instruments), or more exploration of nature. Some outdoor activities—such as carpentry—may only be included at times that a second adult is available to offer close supervision. The teacher can also use the outdoor classroom as the place to snare the interest of those children who blossom outside but seem lost inside—by putting books about bugs in a basket near the rock that always has bugs under it, she can engage the child in meaningful literacy activities, and a few magnifying glasses can lead to scientific inquiry.

Following are lists of materials that can be included in different kinds of outdoor spaces.

Small Spaces

Even a limited space can offer new experiences for the children. Things to add to a small porch or patio:

- A raised planter bed of any size, some seeds, garden tools, and watering cans.
- A paint easel and drying rack that children can use independently.
- A sand/water table with a rotating menu of materials, such as water, sand, oobleck, or other sensory materials noted in Chapter 3. Change the materials when interest begins to flag. Things to add to sand or water may be:
  - small treasures for children to "discover" in the sand
  - measuring cups, funnels, sifters, and spoons, for either sand or water
  - little cars and people or small animals in the sand
  - add water to make wet sand, and implements to sculpt the sand
  - in water, add water wheels, colanders, or little boats
  - items that will sink or float in the water
  - tubes with connectors for older 5s to make pathways for the water
  - dish soap and straws to blow bubbles
  - rubber dolls, soap and washcloths
  - plastic toys that need washing with small scrub brushes and soap
  - food coloring, plastic fish and other sea creatures.

Larger Spaces

If you have more room, add one or more of the following activities:

- A small picnic table for puzzles or small building sets.
- A blanket on the ground with pillows and books.
- Small chairs or a bench with books.

- Musical instruments, hats, and streamers.
- Playground chalk.
- Bubble soap and wands.
- Balls—big ones to bounce, small ones to toss into a box.
- Cardboard boxes to create with (use paint to transform into a train, store, puppet theater, houses).

GENEROUS SPACES

- Paint or chalk-in lines for tricycle/scooter/wagon pathways.
- Low basketball hoops and soft rubber balls.
- Beanbags and balls in a contained area.
- Balance beam and/or climbing equipment.
- Wooden boxes, slide, ladders and boards that can be re-arranged.
- Old sheets or parachutes can be draped over the climber to encourage dramatic play. Bring out props that will add to the "stories" the children are thinking about.
- Simple obstacle courses can be made with planks, short ladders and sawhorses which can be rearranged to offer a variety of challenges. They need to be on grass, sand, or other soft surfaces.
- Low stilts (cans on ropes), or jump ropes.
- Cardboard blocks and a basket of picnic supplies (tablecloth, dishes, cups, and dolls and doll blankets).

USES FOR FENCES AND WALLS

- Small buckets of water and large paintbrushes to "paint" the buildings or fences (younger 4s).
- Clip or tape butcher paper to a fence and provide paints and brushes for a community "mural"—either random pictures or a theme planned by the children (older 5s). (For younger children provide only seasonal colors of paint for a finished product that will be attractive no matter how the drawing works out.)
- Clip one end of a long jump rope to a chain link fence and teach children to jump rope—with an adult turning the rope to match the child's rhythm of jumping.
- Give only one clamp-on roller skate to each child and have them practice skating while holding on to the fence or wall.

TIPS FOR USING ELEMENTARY SCHOOL PLAYGROUNDS

- Use the playground when older children are in class so the young children can have protected access to an appropriate space on the school grounds.

- Invest in a rolling cart to carry equipment outdoors and back.
- Rotate outdoor equipment so that new experiences can be available on different days.
- If some climbing equipment is designed for older children, use orange cones or other clear markers to remind children where they can play safely.
- If only one adult is outdoors with the children, mark off a play area where one person can see everyone, and bring out a phone to call for assistance if needed.
- Water and bathrooms may be far from the play area, so establish the routine of taking everyone to the bathroom first, and keep a water dispenser and paper cups on the cart for children to serve themselves as needed.

Now that the classroom and yards have been carefully designed to engage the children and support the teaching goals, it is time to address the systems needed to support the children's independent use of those spaces.

Routines: The Backbone of Classroom Management

Having routines in place to take care of the mundane tasks in a classroom (where do we put a sweater? what do we do first thing in the morning?) makes the day go more smoothly. In the transitional classroom, one goal is to help children become more independent and manage their own feelings, actions, and learning. Routines teach children how to manage themselves. In the beginning the teacher controls the children, telling them when they can talk, where they should line up, and whose turn it is. A well-designed routine allows the teacher to gradually release that power to the children, as they are ready.

We refer to routines in many contexts and at many levels; they are the systems that underlie every smoothly functioning organization. Throughout the book we will circle back to talk about routines in a variety of contexts. In this section we describe the most basic level, a routine to play with materials, which describes how and where to use a toy or piece of equipment and how to clean up afterward—and the teacher's routine to teach a routine! Another system is the routine of "choosing"—cues that tell the children what is available to choose from. The teacher uses another set of routines to address multi-group instruction—times of the day when the teacher may work directly with a small group while other children play independently. The routine of the schedule cues the children to know when it is time for different types of activities. In the abstract it can sound highly regimented, yet in reality these routines allow the children a lot of freedom to manage themselves.

Young children who may not have been in school before need routines for everything: washing hands, taking out and putting away toys, handling art materials, looking at books on the rug, and anything else the children can do independently. From the practical perspective the goal of routines in the early years is to teach children to be independent in meeting their own needs and caring for the equipment in the classroom. From a larger perspective, routines teach the child how to order and logically structure their thinking and their actions. Finally, young children are striving to feel BIG; managing these everyday tasks without any adult help is the first step to success in the classroom. As they grow, school and life will require ever more logic, order and mental discipline which all begin with learning to follow step-by-step directions independently.

With children coming into the classroom with different abilities to manage themselves, routines have to be taught consistently in a step-by-step fashion. To do this, the teacher must have thought through all the steps carefully to see if they will work before teaching them. Once children have learned to do things one way, it can be difficult to change the habit so it is important to begin teaching the routines on the first day of school. If there is no routine for painting at the easel, for example, children may come up with their own "routines" which do not support your goals. Start with whichever routine you need them to learn right away, and slowly add more as you begin to open different areas of the classroom.

Teaching a Routine for Use of Materials

Here is a simple routine for using table toys:

- Select a toy from the shelf and bring it to the closest table that has a vacant chair. Sit down.
- Play with the toy for as long as you like.
- As soon as you are done, pick up the toy and return it to the shelf. (If it is a puzzle that you did not finish, just put the pieces on top of the puzzle frame before putting it on the shelf.)
- Push in your chair.
- Now you may go choose something else.

The goal is to get the children to follow the steps of the routine without prompting from the teacher. That means each step in the routine has to be cued from the previous step, *not* from an adult saying, "Don't forget to push in your chair." This is accomplished in the following way:

- *First*, the teacher will model or demonstrate how to use table toys to the group—it's fine to do this more than once if needed. Some teachers follow up by choosing several children to also model the routine, and asking the class, "What should she do next?" after each step.
- *Second*, the teacher watches as children follow the routine during playtime. Watch the child's eyes! When the child is beginning to get up from the table, but still looking at the toy, say, "Now put the toy on the shelf." The goal is to

train the child that when they are just disengaging from this play, that is the cue for picking it up and heading for the shelf. If the teacher waits until after the child has forgotten to put the toy away and calls him back, then the cue will be when the teacher calls him back. And that will become the "cue" forever.
- She does the same for each step in the routine: while the child is placing the toy on the shelf and still looking at the shelf, she says, "Now push in your chair." Seeing the toy on the shelf becomes the cue for pushing in the chair, and so on. The good news is that most children in the group will not need this much training—some children remember just from seeing the model. For the few children who can't seem to remember what is expected, the step-by-step cueing approach works best.
- *Third*, the teacher plans her day realistically, so that there will be time to follow through on routine training at the beginning of the school year. Teach only one new routine at a time, while other activities that don't need as much supervision are going on, so that you can focus on thoroughly teaching that one routine. That attention to detail will save more time later, and avoid that feeling of "I've told them a thousand times to …"

This is one reason why the play centers are introduced gradually, so the children can learn how to manage each one independently before more are added. For example, if the teacher has crayons and paper already on one table (no routine needed) and pattern blocks already spread out on another table (no routine needed), she can focus on observing the children who are playing with table toys that have to be put on the shelf.

Routines are meant to be helpful for both the adult and the children, so if there is a routine that is not working well, change it or let it go. Letting children manage the details of the day frees up the teacher to observe the children and engage in higher-level thinking and teaching as she goes through her day.

Routines to Manage Whole Group Instruction

At the beginning of the year, there will be some children who are not developmentally ready to sit in a large group for long, especially in a PreK classroom of 4-year-olds. Whether it is because they are too young and egocentric to care much about being part of a group, or because they are more accustomed to the visual cues of a television, or because they cannot keep their bodies still for any length of time, the remedy is the same: keep whole group time short and weave in opportunities for movement and whole-group response. There will be some who can sit much longer and beg for more stories, and some who cannot sit quietly at all. As the year progresses, the children will become better listeners with practice, and the teacher will also become better at watching for clues to see when it is time to end the lesson. Each class is different, of course, so you may have a "wiggly class" one year and a "quiet class" in another.

One of the first routines you teach will be "coming to the rug." Do children have assigned places, a certain square on the carpet or a number taped to the rug? Do they sit in a circle? Are all the places clearly marked? Assigned places work best in the beginning, as the teacher gets to know the children and arranges them to avoid distracting combinations. Later in the year as the class matures some of these rules may be relaxed, depending on your class.

Some teachers prefer to do whole group instruction at tables, especially with Kindergarteners who may be doing more writing during the lesson. Younger children tend to do better in closer proximity to the teacher. Lightly touching a shoulder, or whispering a child's name, can be done more easily when everyone is on the rug and the less mature children sit closer to the teacher. Even with 5-year-olds, children in the back row of tables or desks can become "lost" in a large classroom and not follow the lesson; putting the more mature and capable students in the back will help.

Whole-group writing without using desks can be done with clipboards or small white boards to write on while on the rug. If children are sitting in a circle so that teacher can see all their white boards, they can practice forming letters, for example, and the teacher can easily see who will need more personal instruction, and can make a note of whom she should work with at another time.

Generally speaking, young children do their best listening first thing in the morning when they are fresh. Many teachers like to take advantage of this by teaching the bedrock academics first in an older class: phonemic awareness, learning the alphabet or sight words, practicing counting and simple math problems, or introducing a new unit of study. These teachers often choose to save other whole-group activities such as calendar, singing, or hearing stories, for later in the day. (If you have a class of young 4s, you can wait to introduce the calendar routines until January—to celebrate the New Year! Or save it for a new activity in Kindergarten, when the children will have a clearer concept of time.)

During the first few weeks of school, when everyone is still getting to know one another, whole group time works much better in several short lessons, rather than in one or two longer ones. With a young class, begin with a 10- or 15-minute lesson, and take your cues from the children as to when they are ready to sit longer. Even a longer lesson can be kept lively and interactive using some of the following techniques:

- Begin with a song that incorporates the names of children who are sitting quietly, ready to learn. This is a very quick way to get everyone's attention.
- Instead of calling on one child to answer a prompt, encourage whole-group response. This works well for short answers (naming a letter or numeral, counting to 20, or repeating classroom rules in unison).

- Use bodily movement in the lesson. Have children stand up (with some space between them) and use whole-body movements to trace letter or numeral shapes in the air, or to demonstrate concepts like "high/low," "fast/slow," etc.
- Intersperse the lesson with a short finger play or song with movement, then go quickly back to the lesson.
- "Simon says …" for about three or four commands, then "Simon says 'time to listen.'" (This works best if it is used sparingly.)
- If you want to call on one child, say, "I'm looking for a quiet person … or a good listener …" to call on. Then call on several "quiet" people to answer the same question.
- Keep the pace lively! Long pauses are an invitation for children's attention to drift away. (Later in the year you may want to have more quiet time on the rug to reflect on a question or to share thoughts with a partner, but this will have to be taught and practiced as the children grow.)
- End the lesson before you lose the children's attention. Watch for signs of restless bodies, eyes staring around the room, or whispering. This will prevent children from "tuning the teacher out" as can happen if the lesson goes on for too long.

Follow these suggestions, or others that your colleagues may have, and the children will learn that the teacher always has interesting things to say, and coming to the rug for a lesson is a fun thing to do. It builds a sense of community in your classroom, and makes the learning feel attuned to the children's interests and capacity.

Routines to Manage Guided Play

Time may be limited for child-initiated play in the first few days of class, but you will be building the foundations that will make more playtime possible. Some of your child-initiated playtime will be used for teaching children how to handle and put away materials that they will later be using independently. Each teacher may have his or her own preference for where to start. Many teachers have had good results by beginning with three easy centers. You will need to plan your space so that one-third of the children can work at each center. (A "center" can be several tables pushed together, or a rug large enough to accommodate that number of children.) The teacher needs to be able to see all three centers at a glance.

If you are already accustomed to having play activities in your classroom, and it works well for you, you may not need this step-by-step guide for training your class to handle themselves independently in the classroom. If you are new to incorporating "play" into your curriculum, or if you would like to make playtime easier to manage for you and the children, you may find the following tips to be helpful.

Begin by introducing the easiest centers (one or two at a time), and go on to introduce new ones only when you see things are going smoothly.

- *Easier* centers are: playdough, math manipulatives, crayons and paper, looking at books, sensory activities, and using table toys (very easy puzzles and manipulatives). Model new centers and teach your routine for beginning free choice time as well as the routine for clean-up—remember that children do not always know how to start or end an activity.
- *More Challenging* centers are those that encourage dramatic play and cooperation, such as the house area and blocks. Introduce these one at a time, saving blocks for last. (You may want to cover the block shelf with butcher paper for the first two or three weeks of school.)
- *Later* you can add activities with more complicated routines, such as painting, using musical instruments, or a listening center.

In the beginning free-choice time will be shorter—but your goal will be to lengthen the time that children can manage and maintain complex play.

Teach children the "freeze" signal before beginning. It may be a bell ringing, the lights blinking, or a "magic word." Practice a few times at the rug before going to the centers. Make it a game!

Introducing the First Three Centers over Three Days

1 **Playdough** (independent)
   Days One and Two have only balls of playdough and mats available (recipe on page 110). Before beginning, show the whole class different ways they can manipulate playdough: pounding, rolling into little balls, rolling to make snakes, poking holes with one's fingers, etc. All these things build fine motor skills. The rule for playdough is that it "stays on the mat." Plastic placemats are ideal, or laminate 12 × 18 pieces of construction paper. (*Unfortunately, store-bought* Play-Doh® *is not ideal for this, because it tends to crumble with heavy classroom use.*)

   On Day Three begin adding new toys to the table—enough for each child *plus a few extras*. Begin with something very simple, such as plastic knives, then vary the center a little each day after that by using different toys. Some that work well are: cylinder blocks for rolling, cookie cutters, garlic presses, tweezers, unusual utensils purchased at a thrift store (check for sharp edges), or small plastic toys or alphabet blocks that can make impressions in the dough. The clean-up routine for playdough is for each child to roll their playdough back into a ball, then put their ball in the plastic container with a lid to keep it fresh for the next child.

> **Why Playdough is Popular with Teachers ...**
> - It allows children of all maturity levels to play together peacefully—children can play independently side-by-side, or they can play cooperatively, making elaborate "cookie stores" or other projects.
> - It is good for helping children release their emotions by pounding, squeezing, or tearing apart the playdough without harming anyone.
> - It develops fine motor skills and can stimulate language development.
> - It is open-ended with endless creative possibilities!
> - It is the ideal activity for that child who is having trouble settling into constructive play. It is not over-stimulating, and there is no "wrong" way to play with it.
> - It is easy to manage and to clean up.

2   **Exploring Math Manipulatives** (independent)
    This is an opportunity for children to explore the manipulatives they will be using later in Kindergarten and first grade. Each day put different ones out: pattern blocks, geo boards, unifix cubes, etc., whatever your school has. Have plenty for everyone at that center! Children can play freely with them as long as they "stay on the table." You can repeat the manipulatives that seem to be most interesting to the children. You can also vary it on successive days by adding counting discs or teddy bear counters. The clean-up for manipulatives is to put them back in the box on the table or rug.

3   **Paper, Crayons, and Scissors** (with teacher supervision and help)
    Begin with some half-sheets of paper, plenty of crayons, and one pair of scissors for each child. Observe how children handle the scissors and teach them as needed. On subsequent days you can vary this table by changing the color of the paper, adding pencils, colored pencils, or erasers. Or, you can pre-cut the paper into circles or triangles, and it becomes a "new" activity. Do not introduce the scissors on the first day, because you may be distracted by whatever is happening at the other two centers. Once you introduce the scissors you may have to demonstrate or help children one-on-one learn to use them. To clean up after cutting, children pick up all the little bits of paper on the table and floor and put them in the recycling basket.

4   **Looking at Books** (another option for beginners—use in place of Paper, Crayons, and Scissors)
    Depending on your class, handling books properly may need to be taught. This is easiest to do in a whole group, perhaps sitting in a circle on the rug. If you use this as your third center, you will be able to work with smaller groups. Have plenty of colorful picture books available, more than one for each child. Children who may not have books at home will need to learn how to

appreciate them. Demonstrate first, by modeling how to turn the pages from the corner and things to notice in the pictures. As the children begin to turn pages in their own books, go around and talk to them about what they see. Books with pictures of animals or children doing things are ideal for this activity.

Managing the Centers

Plan for about an hour for this activity:

- five minutes to demonstrate the playdough to everyone (as when introduced). Divide the children into three groups;
- fifteen minutes at each table; and
- five minutes in between for cleanup and transition.

(On the first day or two, you may only want to plan 10 minutes at each table and a longer time for cleanup and transition!)

Teach the procedure for the transitions. After 10–15 minutes at their first table, children at each table will: (1) tidy up the table for the next group; (2) then stand behind their chairs; (3) FREEZE! While children are "frozen" have the first group walk to the second table and be seated, then the second group to the third table, and the third group to the first table. Only move one group of children at a time! When all are seated, they begin on their next table activity. At first it may seem like you're spending all your time transitioning, but after a few days, children will begin to handle this more skillfully.

Teaching New Activity Centers

Each class is different as to when children are ready for more. Observe your class at the three centers already in use to watch for signs of readiness. When *most* of your group is ready, you can begin free choice. Observe:

1 How well do they follow directions and handle transitions between the three tables?
2 Are they engaged with the activities at the tables and using the materials appropriately?

Now your classroom is ready, and you have made good plans for how to teach the children to use all your interesting materials. You are ready to open the door and start getting to know your class and their parents as well.

Relationships

Building relationships begins with the welcoming smile children see on the teacher's face that first day of school, quickly followed up by the teacher's genuine interest and attention to each child. The best time to get to know each child's strengths and areas for growth are those times when the children are busy at a task and the teacher can step back to observe. It may happen when they are working at tables—drawing, or practice tracing/writing their names—but the most revealing part of the day will be when the children are engaged in guided play. The first week or two of school sometimes feel like a blur of learning names, teaching routines, and helping shy children to find their place in the class or helping more active children settle and focus. However, once the children begin to manage themselves during the play period, some deeper observation can begin. Walk around with a notebook or clipboard with the children's names listed and begin taking notes. Things you might look for are:

- Who is playing with whom? Are they getting along well? Is one child leading, or are they both contributing to the game?
- Who is having difficulty finding a friend or a group to play with? Who is hanging back and having difficulty entering the play?
- Do you notice some children choosing to play alone or just watching as others play?
- Who seems to be more mature (good language skills, interesting ideas, gets along with others)?
- Who seems to be less mature or less experienced at playing with others (not ready to share toys yet, less developed language, fewer ideas of what to do)?
- What skills or talents do you notice? Good fine motor skills? Friendliness? Creativity? Good focus and attention span at what they are doing?
- Look at your class list. Is there someone that seems to slip through the cracks? Is there a child who always seems to be on the edge of things but never stays long?

Often teachers are too busy "teaching" to see what school looks like from the point of view of the child. Sometimes the quiet children can go unnoticed in a busy classroom. As you observe, try to find at least one positive quality that each child has. In some children this is easy to spot, but for others it may not be so obvious. Who is being helpful? Who is good at cleanup? Who is always attentive during whole-group instruction? Then tell the child what you have noticed—though not while they are playing or working on something, because you do not want to interrupt the flow. Transition times are a good time to talk to individual children in passing: "You worked really hard on that puzzle, didn't you?" or "My, you're a good listener!" will go a long way toward building a relationship with that child.

You may have to reach out to shy children who seem to stay below the radar. Ask them about their shoes! (For some reason, 4-year-olds are intensely interested in shoes.) "Who bought you those pink shoes?" may be a conversation starter. Children are much more likely to cooperate with a teacher they like and who likes them.

Most of all, children appreciate a teacher who keeps them safe—physically and emotionally. Step in whenever you see a child who is being teased or excluded in some way. Teach them the words they need to defend themselves ("I don't like that" or "Please stop _____"), and follow through if other children do not respect their wishes.

Most classroom rules boil down to these three:

1   *We Are Safe*
    This rule covers all things dangerous or potentially "not safe." The teacher decides what is not safe and explains why.
2   *We Are Kind*
    This rule includes both physical aggression and hurting another's feelings. Just as you would stop a child who is hitting, you will stop a child who is name-calling or teasing another child. It is best to call attention to how the other child is feeling. "Look at his face," or "He doesn't like your unfriendly words." Next, you must address the source of the problem. Usually the name-caller is feeling pushed or threatened in some way. Teach alternate language they might use, such as:
    • "I'm busy now. I'll play with you later."
    • "I was using this toy first."
    • "Please move—you're in my way."
3   *We Are Responsible*
    This rule addresses the mishandling of equipment and other inappropriate behavior, such as knocking down block towers, breaking crayons, or throwing playdough on the floor. Explain how the materials will be damaged by these actions (for example, the playdough will get dirty) and we need to keep our things nice for other people to use.

First Day of School

It's the first day of school. Some children will waltz into your classroom eager for new experiences, while others will be more hesitant and wary in their approach. Then there are a few—due to their life experiences so far—who are genuinely afraid to be left in a room full of strangers. Often, this can be attributed to the child's temperament (slow to warm up to new situations). Or, it can be due to a mismatch between the culture of home and the culture of school.

Separation anxiety is a normal part of development, which tends to show itself in American culture approaching the age of 2. Most 4- and 5-year-olds will be well past that, but a small percentage of them still experience it. It may be that the child has never been left with someone who is not a family member. It may be that the child lacks experience with other children, and is overwhelmed by so many strange children nearby. In some families, it is the parent who is experiencing the anxiety about leaving their child at school—perhaps their own school experience was not very good. Sometimes, the parents just need reassurance that someone will be paying attention to their child, and that the child has the capacity to manage without the parent.

Every teacher has his own way of easing the transition from home to school. Some teachers take the "cold turkey" approach, feeling that the sooner the parent leaves, the sooner the child will learn to adjust. In many cases, that turns out to be true. Working parents, or parents with other small children, will not be able to stay, so a quick goodbye at the door may be the best option. In a few cases, the child's crying or total withdrawal from activities, may go on for days, or even weeks. This is hard on the other children, as well as the teacher. Meanwhile, weeks of learning may have been missed for that child. Bringing the parent back into the classroom after cutting the ties will only make things worse, as the child might see that as a reward for all the crying. (It should be noted that most children by age 4 will not carry on for *weeks* in a new school, and if that does happen it may indicate that there is another problem with the child's life. The teacher does not need to diagnose it, but might want to start keeping notes in case a later referral is made.)

Some teachers invite the parents in to stay for a while until the child feels more secure. Inviting the parent to stay also has its upside and downside. The best outcome for this approach is that the parent will sit somewhere in a corner while the child joins the group activities, with the child glancing at the corner now and then to reassure herself that a family member is nearby. In this approach, the teacher needs to tell the parent, "Tell me before you leave, so I can help your child say goodbye." When the parent feels ready to leave and tells the teacher, the teacher moves close to the child while the mother says goodbye (hopefully short and sweet!). If the child begins to cry again, the teacher firmly takes the child by the hand, offers comfort, and then helps the child to find a friend or an interesting activity. Many children will settle down if they are given the role of teacher's "helper" with some small task. The teacher's attitude is both friendly and matter-of-fact, and the child soon relaxes and begins to participate.

Parents who tiptoe out without saying goodbye to their child will only cause a more serious problem. From the parent's point of view, this strategy was successful because the parent was not there for the ensuing scene. However, once the child notices what happened, crying or acting out will increase because the child's trust in their parent has been broken, and who knows what might happen next? Will the teacher also abandon me? It can take days or weeks for this trust to be regained.

Another outcome for this approach could be to prolong the separation. The teacher may discover that the child is fine, after a while, but the parent still wants to stay. How does the teacher know when is the best time for the parent to leave? Once the child becomes involved in an activity or is talking to the other children, he is probably ready to be left. The teacher tells the parent what she observed, and suggests the parent can leave now. Or, would the parent like to stay and be a helper?

This is a win–win outcome. Either the parent will say goodbye to the child and leave without difficulty, or the teacher will now have a volunteer in the classroom, where there is plenty to do. Part of preparing for the first day of school may be to have some unfinished projects in the corner that a parent can work on. Other things a parent can do on the first day of school is sit at a table activity and keep the children focused on what they are doing, help a less able child to complete a task, prepare a snack, or help with cleanup. Giving parents specific tasks will keep them from hovering over the child (if that seemed to be the issue) and to make them feel needed. Teachers who are comfortable with parent helpers may even invite some parents to stay and help if they would like to!

Helping Children to Make Friends

After several weeks of school, most children will have found their niche. However, there may be one or two children who still seem not to be fitting in. Teaching children how to build good relationships with others is one of the teacher's responsibilities in a child-centered program. In typically developing children, there are distinct stages of social development, though the ages may vary with individual children:

1 The infant bonds with its primary caretaker: the first relationship.
2 Toddlers can play near other children, but not too closely! They do not yet understand that other people have feelings too, and they may see other children as interesting playthings. They enjoy imitating other children and getting attention from them, but cannot share or reciprocate in play.
3 Preschoolers (beginning at 2½ or 3) make friends and like to play with or near other children, but still can only see the world from their own point of view. They are often surprised to learn that other children have feelings too. At the younger range in this stage, they play best if they can each have their own toys and play side-by-side. As they mature, they begin to play in small groups, but each child will have a different game in her head. For example, there may be a house with a Mommy, and Doctor, and a Waitress, each one happily making up their own game as they go along.
4 In the transitional phase (beginning at about 4½ or 5) children begin to be more interested in making friends than they are in owning the toys. This is when true sharing begins, as they begin to listen to each other's ideas and cooperate. At this stage children can be taught to "take turns" with a game or a toy, but true sharing must always come from the child's desire to be part of

a group. If "sharing" is imposed by adults before the children are ready, it becomes "compliance" rather than sharing from the heart.
5   Older 5s and 6-year-olds are usually quite good at cooperative dramatic play, where everyone has a role, and all players are following the same "script" (taking a sick baby to the hospital, going to a restaurant, or having a picnic in the park). However, they still struggle with games that have rules, and may need some adult supervision as they learn to play board games, for example.
6   Beginning at about age 7 or 8, children enter a new phase of development, when they will be able to play their positions in team sports and follow the rules in more organized group games without quite as much adult supervision.

It is helpful to keep this gradual progression of social skills as a backdrop when looking at a child's social development. Children's progress through the stages depends just as much on prior experience as it does on their age. Children with little experience playing with other children may seem to be at a less mature stage than their age may indicate. The good news is that—given the opportunity to practice—those children will progress more quickly to the next stage, because of the maturity of their brains.

Figure 2.7 Children connect through play
Source: Photo courtesy of Geraldine Rocha.

Success breeds success in learning. The first step in helping that child is to see what kind of play the child is already able to manage without help. Build on the success that has already been made by making small changes in that child's environment that will encourage the next stepping stone. Depending on where the child's development is, the teacher can try the following interventions:

- Does the child always play alone? Is there another child who could be persuaded to play next to that child? Look for someone who enjoys the same kind of toys as the child who plays alone. Talk to them in a friendly way about what they are doing, to see if they can begin to notice each other.
- Does the child watch other children playing? Find out which activities the child finds most interesting, and set up a small space where that child can play next to another child with similar toys.
- Is the child already playing near another child, but without interacting? Chances are they will soon discover each other. However, the teacher can help by talking about what each of them are doing or asking them to talk about it. This may awaken their interest in what the other child is thinking.
- Is the child too shy to enter a group, but stays nearby observing the play? Often inexperienced players do not know what to do or say, but they want to interact with others. The teacher can step in with a prop that gives that child an entrée into the group. One excellent prop is an empty pizza box. The teacher may prompt the child to knock at the door of the playhouse and say, "Your pizza is here!" Often that is all that is needed, and the "delivery person" is invited to stay and eat, too. Or, the teacher may need to say "The pizza man has a delivery for you!" and help things proceed from there. If the group does not want the pizza, the teacher can coach them to say, "Bring it back later." Then on the second attempt the group will be more likely to say "Yes." Another good prop is a mailbag with letters in it (a great use for your junk mail!). A socially immature child can carry it around the room giving mail to one and all. These positive interactions (who doesn't want to see their mail?) will help build confidence in the shy child.
- Does the child want to enter into group play but is often rejected by the group? Watch that child's social approach. Inexperienced children tend to barge into play without asking, or take toys from another child. Children with a poor social approach will often respond well to some coaching from the teacher: "Ask them if you can play," is a good start for 5s. (With 4s, that question may just invite a loud "NO!" Four-year-olds will do better with the sort of entry suggested above, with the child entering play by adding a new dimension and role to it.) If the group seems unwilling, have them respond politely by saying, "We're busy now. You can play with us later." If the group lets the child play, stay to help that child find an acceptable role in the play. "Who is he going to be?" "Where is his space?" are important decisions the

group must make before the teacher leaves. Giving the child a prop that fits the role the group has given him will help the child remember how he fits into this group.

Another scenario when a child needs help in finding a friend is when someone joins the class in the middle of the year. Sometimes the newcomer will jump right in, but other children may not be that confident. This is a good time to choose one of your more mature, responsible children to take charge and be the new child's "helper" for the day. Explain exactly what you would like them to do: play with him at recess, show him where to stand in line, help him get through the cafeteria line, introduce him to your friends. Five-year-olds love to do this, and by the second day, the new child is usually integrated into the classroom. Four-year-olds may need more support in this role, but at least they will have a friendlier attitude toward the new child if given the responsibility.

In most cases, a little help at the right time will solve the problem of the "friendless" child. In rare cases where you have persistently tried to intervene and one child still seems to not engage socially with anyone, it may be time for a parent conference to get more background on the child. In any case, the teacher should start keeping notes with dates and incidents noticed in case a referral needs to be made later.

Communicating Your Teaching Practice to Parents

This blended teaching through play and instruction is often confusing to parents, as well as principals and teachers of upper grades, so they may need you to interpret what is underneath the play they see in your classroom. You will become the translator, helping them to interpret what they are seeing and understand why it is important for their child's success in school. Your work as "translator and explainer" of your program begins before school starts, as you create signs for your interest centers, informative bulletin boards, and handouts to give parents on the first day of school.

The recent brain research discussed in Chapter 1 has shown that most 4-year-olds are not yet ready for Kindergarten, and most 5-year-olds are not yet ready for the rigors of first grade. There have also been studies that show how guided play helps brains develop more neural connections at this critical time in development, and gives children some life skills that cannot be taught by direct instruction. These skills include self-regulation (self-control), social skills, bodily coordination, multitasking, problem solving, and creativity, to name a few. All of these are important for success in school and in life. Some of the information in Chapter 1 may be very interesting to parents who want to understand how you are supporting their child's development.

Other parents are less interested in research and more interested in knowing: "Does my child like school?" "Is the teacher well-informed?" "Is the classroom well-managed?" "Are essential skills being taught?" and "Will my child be ready for first grade?"

Some teachers begin the year by posting a sign that reads:

PLAY = Purposeful Learning All Year

and then back it up with signs at each interest center that lists the academic and personal skills that are practiced in that area. We have included examples of such signs in Appendix 2 which you are welcome to copy and post in your classroom if you choose to.

Post your daily schedule where parents can see it and list the "Learning Outcomes" of each block of time. For the times labeled "Guided Play" list some of your goals for the group, or refer parents to the signs you have posted at each center. Also be sure to mention (early and often) that you will also be giving direct instruction in pre-reading and pre-math skills and assessing children's progress in these areas. Say to parents: "We believe academics are very important, and your child will definitely learn reading and math because we are laying the foundation for literacy and numeracy in our program."

Be sure to include on your schedule a daily story time (or two) when you will be reading high quality children's literature to the class. (See more about this in Chapter 4.) The learning goals here include listening skills, general knowledge about the world, and enriching vocabulary. The importance of good literature cannot be overemphasized. Books use literary language, which is not usually found in conversation. When children are exposed to these words early on, they have a distinct advantage that begins to show itself in the upper grades. Academic vocabulary is a gateway skill to success in high school and college.

In answer to specific questions, here are some sound bites that may help parents understand how and why "guided play" is a learning activity:

- We are using guided play, rather than free play, because the teacher's guidance is important for children to get the most out of their play experience. I am observing and helping them to be successful in carrying out their ideas.
- Play is important for language development: children learn more language while they are playing with peers, because their friends need more explanations to understand a playmate's ideas, whereas adults can "fill in the blanks" when children talk to them.
- Play, when infused with opportunities to interact with letters and numbers (such as alphabet puzzles or games with numbers) has been shown to prepare children for early literacy and numeracy.

- Play is an opportunity to practice critical thinking, and problem solving as children set problems for themselves, then solve them.
- Play teaches children to think creatively—"outside the box."
- Block play gives children a deep understanding of Euclidian space (shapes, sizes, and relationships) which will show up as better math skills in middle school and high school. (Many of the benefits of play show up later in life.)
- Dramatic play enhances children's phonemic awareness and concentration, as children must filter out the background noise and focus on what their playmates are saying. Phonemic awareness is a high predictor of success in reading.
- Dramatic play also enhances "story sense" as the children create their own dramatic scenarios. By playing out their stories, the children are gaining an intuitive sense of sequence of events, setting, and plot, which they will need to understand literature (another skill for the upper grades).
- Play teaches life skills: love of learning, self-control, how to work collaboratively, and how to peacefully resolve conflicts.
- Play develops the brain's Executive Function when a child holds multiple threads of complex social play in his head at the same time.
- According to Einstein, "Play is the highest form of research." (This is why innovative tech companies encourage their employees to "play" in the workplace.)

Culturally Responsive Relationships with Children and Families

In the beginning of the year the teacher may occasionally remark "There is so much to learn at school, isn't there? That's okay, we are all learning about that and sometimes we make mistakes when we're learning. Soon you'll remember to keep your hands back while you ask to use a toy that someone else is using." This teacher's friendly support is establishing the culture of her classroom.

The classrooms and play yards of the primary grades are protected; they offer real life experiences that are just the right size for young children, so they can practice and manage the difficult situations that come up in their world. By helping children to handle situations that are difficult for them, and by protecting them from the big adult world that is beyond their comprehension or capacity to manage, the teacher creates a reliable, trusting community which becomes a safe base for experimentation and openness to learning. Creating a community where children are protected from adult worries beyond their capacity to understand, let alone manage, is a socially constructive way to support healthy development. A gradual increase in the responsibilities and concerns handed to a child, in balance with his capacity to understand and manage them, creates a resilient adult who is confident that he can weather whatever stresses life brings.

Community reflects culture, and culture is embedded in education. The goals we set for children reflect our culture, and the environment in which the children are immersed is established by the adults who are preparing the children to take their places in that culture. While we acknowledge that young children are not developmentally ready to understand racial and income inequities, glass ceilings, or other social justice issues, we also acknowledge that they live in a culture that includes all of that. The piece of influence we have as teachers is in the small world of our classrooms, where we will maximize our impact to see that every child receives what he or she needs to thrive in this culture, and hopefully to shape it for the better.

Perhaps the most challenging part of teaching tolerance and inclusion is that each of us is immersed in our own culture and inevitably looking through that lens. One's own culture is as invisible to oneself as another person's culture is obvious. Culture also changes as society changes; there was a time when girls in America had to wear dresses to school; now there are few limitations on clothing for either sex, as long as the child is decently covered. Self-awareness, reflection and openness to alternative ideas and thoughts diversify and expand not only one's own capacity for inclusion but the very culture we are creating at this moment. So today we look at ourselves and ask how our beliefs fit into our culture, and how do we want to live our lives and our values? I can choose to approach the world from my heart, or my mind, or both. With awareness of my own experiences as well as those of others, how will I be sensitive to gender stereotypes, religion, family, and the value of material goods? What is the culture I am creating in my classroom for my children?

In 1916 John Dewey, the father of American education, wrote "Education is a social process; education is growth; education is not preparation for life but is life itself." Dewey held teachers responsible for much more than delivering the curriculum—their job included the responsibility to teach social norms and to establish an interactive community of learning in the classroom. Dewey advocated for social reform, believing that the correction of many social ills could and should begin in the schools. Dewey and his colleagues were working early in the 20th century with many of the same challenges that are in our schools today—immigrant populations, second language learners, children entrenched in generations of deep poverty and despair, and those suffering from racism, displacement and cultural exclusion.

Dewey believed that an intentional teacher could begin to help the children see and learn social alternatives within the culture of a thoughtful classroom experience. In the classroom the teacher can insist that words carry more power than physical aggression, that all people are treated fairly, and that gender is irrelevant to achievement. She can model the curiosity and interest in learning that keep us growing. The teacher who believes that kindness and friendship are essential skills will transmit those values to the children in her classroom. Even as children still struggle to use language to express their strong emotions at school, many parents have related a story in which the child's experience at school began to influence her broader culture when she reminded someone in her family, or at the park, that she would rather they tell her what they need in a friendly voice. The intentional teacher sets up her classroom as a place full of options and alternatives to think about and frame social and cultural norms.

Knowing that the only true constant is change, teachers establish a classroom culture that teaches inclusion, flexibility and acceptance in all interpersonal relationships while creating predictability, stability and order through rules and procedures in the classroom. The order and the rules provide the framework for the children within which they can focus on developing their interpersonal relationships. Just as traffic laws allow freedom to each driver within a framework of agreements about the rules of the road, the rules and structure give freedom and opportunities for more and greater learning opportunities to the children. If we believe boys and girls are equal, rules must be enforced equally and individualization of rules and consequences must be explained in the context of meeting each person's needs rather than because of stereotypes. "*JJ had better go out for a quick run around the climber; he'll be able to sit and listen better when he comes back. Go quick, JJ, and come right back. Anne, you better go out for a quick run too; you have been sitting still so long working on words that I think your body needs a break from thinking so hard.*"

True learning about inclusion comes through the teacher's warmth, acceptance, and openness modeled for the children. To teach children to believe that all people are created equally we embrace and welcome each child as an individual, each one a unique combination of family, religion, language, socio-economic group, color, custom and culture. The more the children see the teacher's caring and respect for the parents, the more the teacher will be loved by the children and the more the parents will love having the child at school.

Thinking up activities to demonstrate and include children in each other's differences (such as holidays) are easy but easily become clichéd. Children feel affirmed, included and welcomed when the teacher includes pictures of people who look like themselves and have families like theirs, as well as displaying the multitude of other ways one can form a fine family, in the décor on the walls and books on the shelf. Some teachers ask families to bring in pictures of children with their other family members, putting them all together on a common shelf or bulletin board for everyone to share and enjoy. Toys from diverse cultures can be added to the dress-up and cooking areas as long as they make sense to the children; if no one has ever seen anyone cook with a cooking gourd it will not be used well, but if children are familiar with a wok in the kitchen it would be a good addition. Clothing too needs context: if the children do not see men from Myanmar wearing their long skirts, adding them to the dress-up area could bring more confusion than understanding.

Because the brain hunts for difference, choosing to focus on similarities will help the children see the oneness in humanity. "Everyone is different and everyone is the same" speaks to the age-old understanding that while we each have our own unique qualities we are also very similar. We all have grown-ups who love and care for us, we all have favorite things we love to eat, we all feel sad sometimes, we all like to laugh. It can be a good literacy activity as well as a social activity to let the children brainstorm a list. It can become a math activity too, if in a follow-up children self-identify subsets within those groups. For example, "we all have grown-ups who love and care for us" can be broken out into sets of who those grown-ups are in each house—mom, dad, two moms, mom and dad, grandma and dad, etc. Focusing on these similarities in the big picture, and differences in the small one, teaches tolerance, inclusion, and understanding.

One of the challenges to consider as we bring cultural inclusion into a 4- and 5-year-old classroom is that it coincides with brains that are developmentally very busy sorting and ordering everything, getting ready to move into more categorical thought patterns. Teachers often hear children sorting each other "Only girls with brown skin sit here. Boys with dinosaurs on their shirts get the big shovels. Only kids with two moms get to be in the show. Big sisters with babies get to climb to the top of the climber." This is just sorting to the 4-year-old, but our adult experiences with racism, sexism, privilege and political correctness leap to the forefront of our thinking. When children are engaged in this spontaneous premath, sorting and making sets, take a step back and check to be sure of the context before stepping in. If "Only the brown girls climb now" is followed by "Ok, now it is the pink girls' turn" you may check the children's faces to see if anyone is disturbed by the game, and if not just go on with your business. If anyone seems left out, the teacher can ask the children to tell her more about their game and look for an opportunity to discuss whose feelings might be hurt and why. As she does this, she will avoid jumping to any assumptions based on her adult experiences, and stay open to true understanding of the thinking going on in these immature brains.

As we reflect on these concepts and reflect on our own character development we are aware that our relationships with parents as well as co-teachers and classroom helpers must also fit into the picture of who and how we relate to one another. The more welcomed and valued a parent feels, the more likely it is that their child will be happy in your classroom. When the parents feel safe and included, their attitudes will let their child know that you, your classroom, and the school are safe for them. Attendance will improve because the family believes their child is getting something valuable from participating in your classroom, and any resistant behavior should diminish.

Being friendly with parents does not mean becoming the parent's friend; it simply means sharing your knowledge of their child with them in a kind, friendly, professional way. Being warm and open, choosing to be happy rather than scolding when you see them straggling in late; saying "Oh, you made it! I'm so glad you are here," shows the parents that you are kind, thoughtful and caring as you go about your job.

The only possible downside to a relaxed and friendly relationship with parents is that they may look for your support when you are busy with your class. If you are busy helping the class when a parent thinks you are available to chat, tell him directly "I need to attend to the children now; I'm teaching them to work together so I need to listen to what they say to each other. Can you write down a number where I can call you around 2 this afternoon?" In that brief message the parent learned more about how you teach, and how seriously you take your relationship with the children—including their child—and that you do want to hear what he has to say as well. Another morning a frazzled parent may want to discuss problems with her child's behavior right at the door, yet you do not want to talk about a child over his head, knowing he hears every word and this jeopardizes his perception of safety in his relationship with you. When the parent starts in—"Gray is in big trouble, he bit his sister last night"—have some handy de-escalating comments at hand: "Oh, Ms. Posato, thanks for telling me about what an upsetting evening you all had; it must have been a tough night. Gray, do you want a hug goodbye? Then you can come right over to the drawing table to start your day drawing some of that mad out. Ms. Posato, let's set up a time to talk when we can have time for a good conversation." Building an honest relationship with parents will serve you well if you find yourself needing to have a difficult conversation with the parent, and will help the child moving through the school.

Parenting is not easy; young children are difficult to understand and to keep up with. All parents want their children to be loved and be successful, and they want to feel proud of their child. The child in your class may be their ray of sunshine in an otherwise difficult, stressful world; this child may be the best thing they have going for them. The more emotionally present the parents can be for their children, the better it is for both the children and the parents. The more good things you can find to tell the parents about their child, the more you build the parent–child relationship. Even when that child is out of your classroom and off school property, the more he feels loved the better he will do in class. The teacher's kindness and support to the adults in the children's lives can make a big difference in the quality of life in her classroom.

Parent Conferences: Two-Way Conversations

All parents are intensely interested in their child's progress and development. Their job is to be their child's advocate and emotional support as he enters school. PreK and Kindergarten may be the first point of contact with the educational system for parents. First-time parents are learning about school (which may be very different from the school they remember from their own childhood) and also learning about how their child copes with this new environment. They want their child to succeed in school and in life, and they rely on compassionate teachers to help them understand and function in this new world.

Beginning with this view of parents, the teacher's job is to reassure and support new parents, as well as to give them a realistic picture of their child's strengths and areas of concern. Parenting styles differ widely with the life style and education that parents have been exposed to, but they all rest on the premise above: parents want what they believe is best for their own precious child. Upwardly mobile parents may insist that their child get more homework, whereas working parents with two or three jobs between the two of them may not have time to supervise homework. Parents who had negative experiences in their own schooling may avoid coming in to talk to the teacher. Parents born and educated in another country may need a mini course on American education—they may especially need to know that in America it is considered appropriate for parents to speak up for their children if they feel something is being overlooked. Parents who are already overwhelmed by other family issues (marital problems, substance abuse, unemployment, or serious illness—which can affect families of any socio-economic level) might not be able to address problems their child is having in class. Parents who are insecure about their own parenting can come off as defensive … the list goes on. Whether you are meeting with relaxed and confident parents whose child is doing well in school, or worried parents whose child needs extra support, you can use the conference to gain more insight into the child's life at home. It is especially important that the teacher prepare carefully for conferences, so that she will continue to build a relationship with parents that establishes her as a trusted partner in their child's development and education.

Children who are having serious problems in the classroom are likely to also be having them at home. Their conference should begin the same way all parent conferences do, on a positive note about the child's good qualities, talents, or habits. (If you have not noticed any of these qualities, make a point of observing that child more closely until you find them—even if you have to watch her at lunch or recess.) Your next job is to ask questions and listen: What does your child like to do at home? Does she play with other children? What do you see as her strong points?

With this positive beginning, then you can move to the topic of concerns. Often a good way to approach this is to share some information from the developmental charts at the end of this book. Many parents have no one with whom to compare their child, and no real idea of where they are developmentally. If they seem delayed for their age, it may be lack of experience or practice. Be ready with a few practical suggestions, such as inviting a friend over after school, letting her pick out picture books at the library and reading together more often, or getting more outdoor exercise. If the parent is genuinely under so much stress that these things are not practical, be prepared with information on social services that might help: affordable counseling, Al-Anon meetings, or parent resources through the school district. Most schools have already developed a list of resources; if not, it would be a good project to work on.

Often it is the earliest contact with school that uncovers special needs in a child's development. The PreK teacher has the most difficult job, that of being the first person to give the parent this unwelcome news. The parent may be in denial or even angry at the messenger, but take the long view: this parent will hear the same thing again in Kindergarten, and again in first grade. About the third time a different teacher brings it up, the parent will be ready to listen and get the needed help. Leaving this problem for the next teacher to deal with robs that child of a vital year of early intervention that could help improve her chances for a successful life.

Another way to approach this sticky issue is to invite another professional to attend the conference as well: the speech therapist, a school counselor, an experienced colleague, or an administrator. Plan the conference together with that person. It is helpful if that person has been able to observe or assess the child before meeting with the parent. No matter who is there, the conversation should always begin with the positive and be sensitive to what the parent is going through.

Once rapport has been established, parents and teachers can become powerful allies in making changes for the benefit of the child. A parent who chooses to work with the teacher will stay in communication about successes and setbacks, and the teacher can become a valuable support person for the parent—someone who sees what is special about that child and shares in small victories. Yes, all of this takes extra time and preparation, and the rewards are worth it.

Working with Aides, Parents, and Volunteers

Other adult helpers in the classroom can be both a gift and a challenge. At the top of the list are paid assistants or teacher's aides. A compatible, sensitive, and energetic teacher's aide who comes in every day at the same time and gets to know the children is on the "gift" end of the spectrum: the more you have communicated with him your goals, philosophy, and routines, the more helpful he will be. Begin by ascertaining that person's strengths, both by asking what he likes to do and by observing him in action with the children. In the beginning you may spend some time teaching him about your classroom norms and modeling how you would like things done. Finding the time to train a new person is the "challenge" side of the equation, but the results make it worthwhile.

More information is usually better than less, as long as confidentiality is not an issue: you may want to brief your assistant on how to handle a particular child who is having difficulty settling down, or your goals for the shy child who is not yet playing with others. If possible, take time near the beginning of your relationship to answer questions, and to explain why, for instance, you are modulating your voice as you talk to the children (because children will imitate the teacher's tone of voice, and it will make the room quieter) or other habits that you notice. Once you and your frequent helper are working well together, you will fall into routines that both of you are comfortable with: while you are giving whole group instruction your aide may be preparing a snack or sitting with a child who has difficulty listening in a group—whichever is needed most. The teacher is the one who is able to do everything in the job description, so things usually run more smoothly when the aide is doing the things he does best.

Another resource, if you work in an elementary school, is upper-grade helpers. In many ways they are easier to work with than adults, because they are used to following teacher directions. They enjoy reading stories to a small group, or helping children to learn how to jump rope on the patio. The caveat with student helpers is that some of them want to come in and play with the children. This is worse than unhelpful, as it prevents children from developing their own ideas for play and learning how to solve their own problems. A better time for these young helpers to come in is during the modified playtime described in Chapter 3, where they can supervise a board game at a table with four children, or sit at a special art project, such as helping the children peel crayons to do leaf rubbings.

Parent helpers come with an assortment of skills, experiences, and attitudes, but most parents want particularly to see how their own child is doing in school. Near the beginning of the year, there may be a number of "helpful" parents popping in. For these new parents, you want them to have a positive experience without having to invest a lot of time training them. Begin by being welcoming, but also be ready with a specific task for a first-time parent helper to do. Some things that most parents can do well are:

- Sit down in a quiet corner with one child and read a counting book with her, helping her point to each object as they count together.
- Sit at a table and run a Bingo game with four or five children. Avoid discipline problems by beginning with children who are usually cooperative. If that person becomes a regular helper, she can learn how to handle other children as well.
- Some parents are most comfortable doing housekeeping tasks such as preparing and cleaning up after snack. If there is a messy art project going on, this is the ideal person to put at the art table with a sponge and a wastebasket to help things stay neat—but be sure that he knows the limits and that the children are free to use the materials as they like within those limits.
- Perhaps the help you need at the beginning of the year is secretarial: putting together a class set of journals for the children to "write" in (remembering that drawing—even scribbling—is really pre-writing!). Or you may want someone to cut up colored paper for a special art project. Seat the parent at a back table where she can watch the children as she does this task.
- If you work at a school where many parents like to help in the classroom, you will want to have a sign-up sheet outside your door with specific times and jobs listed. Once you have more than two parents in the room at the same time the extra "help" can become distracting for both you and the children.
- Some parents truly want to be helpful, but cannot come into the classroom for a variety of reasons. You can offer to give them some art paper to cut into shapes, for example, or other paperwork to do at home and bring back to you by a specific date.

- Finally, if you are unfortunate enough to have a parent volunteer who behaves inappropriately (smoking, yelling at children, distracting the class from their work, or bringing other children with them, for example) you must firmly but politely tell them that there is a "school policy" against those things and they need to stop what they are doing or leave and come back at another time.

A parent or other adult who is naturally good at working with children is another gift—the grandpa who offers to start a vegetable garden on your patio, the mother who is a consummate storyteller, or the father who can show the children how bread is made—will open windows for the children to see into the wider world around them. It is really worth the reformatting needed in your curriculum to work these unexpected gifts into your plans.

The year is launched, children are learning the systems and routines that give them freedom in your classroom, and you are getting to know each of their strengths and areas needing your support. In Chapter 3 we will go deeper into the subtleties of teaching that make it an art as much as a science.

Reflection on Chapter 2

During the first month of school you were preparing your classroom for active learning, teaching your students some beginning routines, and getting to know the families that you will be working with this year. Take a few moments to look back and assess where you are in this process:

1. Is your room working the way you would like it to?
   Which parts work the best at meeting both the children's needs and your own?
   Are there any parts that you feel are still a "work in progress"? If so, what resources do you need to make improvements?
2. How well are your students doing at following routines?
   Which routines seem to go smoothly? Why do they work so well?
   (*Some things that make routines work well are: there is adequate space and time for children to follow each step; each step leads smoothly to the next step; children have had an opportunity to practice this routine.*)
   Are there any routines that are more problematic? If so, why do you think that is?
   (*Some things that can hamper a smooth routine are: crowding or bottlenecks that cause children to have to wait their turn; there are too many steps in the routine; or children are not able to go at their own pace through each step.*)

3. Take a look at your class list. As you read each name, picture that child in your head and notice any feelings you may have: positive, negative, or indifferent. This is a way to make yourself aware of children whom you still need to find a connection with. How will you make that connection?

   (*One way teachers can connect with students is to watch that student in particular for a day or two, noticing what they like to do, how the other children treat them, and what incidents make them happy, angry, or sad. Another way is to invite parents to tell you more about what the child is like at home.*)

Chapter 3

Guiding and Growing the Whole Child

Key Information in this Chapter
- Refining the systems of routines and transitions
- Adding skills to teach through play
- Developing each play area of the classroom
- Introducing modified play

Teaching is both an art and a science. The art is about how the teacher blends the science—knowledge of development, needs of individual children, curriculum goals and developmental goals—to gracefully and appropriately meet each child's needs. The teacher who masters this art carries learning far beyond the curriculum, and into the hearts and minds and lives of the children. The teacher's academic understanding of his work, his awareness of the children's stage of development, and the influence of the various children's temperaments and experiences on their learning is the science that can be studied. Assembling all that data and analyzing it through the lenses of creative, flexible, forward thinking leads to an artfully crafted classroom full of learning opportunities the children cannot resist. The teacher's observations, which lead to reflection and flashes of inspiration, culminate in the creation of a clever activity that draws the children together and creates shared community, growth, and understanding. This deeper, broader thinking is facilitated by a strong framework of systems (the room, routines and relationships covered in Chapter 2) that give the child and the teacher the freedom to explore, think and grow. This chapter is full of tips and systems that will help you wholly enjoy the process of finding the master teacher lurking within you.

Looking at the eager faces of the children, the teacher can feel how proud and ready the children are to be part of the learning community he is creating in his classroom. They are proud to be big, to be independent and to learn about being in school, along with being excited and a little nervous. The teacher, knowing that the children are stepping into a new and different understanding of themselves and their world, has the job of maintaining this enthusiasm while also channeling it. In the first weeks the teacher will begin to feel the rhythm and pace of the children and the day. There will be an ebb and flow through the year; after a few weeks the excitement and enthusiasm will wane a bit as the children feel a bit overwhelmed by all the new people and rules and spaces they encounter ... and then some weeks later the enthusiasm will surge again with new friends made and challenging projects capturing the children's imagination. It is comforting and predictable for teaching to follow the schedule and curriculum plans, but it will be the teacher's creative spark, and his knowledge of both teaching and children, that will keep the class learning and moving forward.

The Teacher's Role in Guiding Play

Unlike "free play," guided play (or teacher-facilitated play) assumes that the teacher has definite learning goals for the children aligned to their development. These goals will be a little different for every child (see Individualized Goals later in this chapter) depending on their needs and stage of development.

The general goals for 4-year-olds are:

- Learning how to choose an activity (showing initiative)
- Learning how to start and stop an activity
- Engaging in play (rather than wandering or only observing)
- Learning how to play near or with others harmoniously (respecting their space and materials)
- Taking responsibility for cleaning up their area
- Increasing their attention span as they grow
- Using words to express their needs and feelings
- Listening to others' needs and feelings
- Learning to control strong feelings and self-regulate
- Regulate energy level (speed up for recess, and slow down for story).

Note that achieving these goals requires the teacher's support and guidance; this is another reason that 4-year-olds are best supported in classrooms with more than one teacher.

For 5-year-olds, start with the above goals if they have not yet been mastered. In addition, goals for 5-year-olds include:

- Learning how to play cooperatively in a group (children become willing to compromise for the sake of the group play)
- Refining the language they use with peers, with some care for their feelings
- Increasing their engagement and persistence in more complex play (larger groups, more complicated creations, desire to carry a theme over to another day)
- Finding or making materials they need to use as props for their play (initiative and creativity), including going to other areas of the room to find what they need
- Interest in making signs to label their creations (with teacher help).

As one goes deeper into understanding children in the PreK and Kindergarten age, one realizes how functional behavior is and how much meaning it carries. The teacher's challenge is to uncover the meaning behind the behavior and interpret it into words that can provide the child with the language he needs to control his actions and behave in socially acceptable ways. Expressing his needs and feelings in words will eliminate the need to act them out. In fact, an important part of the PreK and Kindergarten teacher's agenda is helping the children to make this transition from the more non-verbal-acting-out of feelings to internalizing self-control and communicating with language. By the end of the Kindergarten year, typically developing children should be able to achieve this goal with the teacher's guidance and support. Teaching these skills that move the inexperienced and immature child forward is a requirement rather unique to the PreK and Kindergarten teacher. Rather than a credential based in curriculum subject matter, the PreK/K teacher needs a credential based on the subject matter of the child himself. Teachers of young children need a broad understanding of child development, the influence of temperament, and strong communication skills to guide the child through this transition toward school-age thinking and behavior. In addition, the PreK and Kindergarten teachers must engage all the domains through which the child is learning to successfully individualize and scaffold the child's learning. The mind, body and spirit of the young child are integrating these human qualities into the wholeness we see in the older child.

Young children begin learning entirely through the body; you can see toddlers almost "become" the truck they are pushing, or the dolly's mommy. Thoughts are processed externally by verbalizing them; the constant flow of talk from children at play shows their inability to hold and process thoughts inside the mind. Just as beginning readers must say the written word aloud before reading silently, thoughts too are spoken aloud until they can be held in the mind. Ideally the children in PreK and Kindergarten are nearing the end of the transition from action to thought, and with reminders and opportunities to practice they will soon integrate all the domains of their learning quite naturally. In the process of achieving that, you will see that the children are drawn to a primary focus on understanding their relationships with each other. This is the way children this age were designed to learn long before schools existed—they learned from each other, experimenting with words and actions.

This need to relate to each other is why children need long periods of time in the classroom for guided play. It is how children develop social skills, self-regulation and cooperation skills; although they are not fields of study like reading or math, all these skills are paramount in the development of the foundation from which academics are learned. Whether they play with blocks, playdough, jump ropes or dolls, children learn how to talk and listen to other children, and will work to moderate their own behavior in order to sustain play that engages them. Once they have attained the skills to sustain a friendship, they will be ready to shift their focus to learning from the teacher's agenda. It is helpful to realize that this drive to be and have a friend is a biological need hard-wired into the brain for the survival of the species, so rather than try to argue with human development, teachers might as well help the children address this natural urge—then they can easily move on to an academic agenda.

Dramatic play in the blocks, the dollhouse, art, and music are all opportunities that engage and teach the whole child, and provide the teacher openings to step in and guide social and emotional competence. This chapter will extend and support you in this process, which began when you set up your classroom in the beginning of the year.

Observing and Assessing

The teacher of young children is constantly multi-tasking: putting a Band-Aid on a skinned knee while checking to see if the rest of the class is on track; setting a calming hand on one child's shoulder while reading a story to the group; or answering the phone while supervising the children preparing for lunch. Nowhere is this multi-tasking more evident than when the teacher is guiding constructive play.

Once the year is under way and the teacher has assessed her class and set some goals for individual students, guided play becomes the most challenging and/or the most rewarding part of the day. During guided play the teacher is keeping three important balls in the air:

1   observing
2   assessing individual children
3   guiding the play.

Observation is the cornerstone skill in this trio: observing how the children are playing will inform the teacher when or where some guidance is needed to keep the play constructive. Noticing skills in individual children will inform the teacher about strengths and skills to work on. Carrying around a clipboard with a class list on it, or a pad of sticky notes to jot down thoughts on individual children, can be helpful in setting goals for their development.

Things to notice during guided play include:

- *Student engagement:* Are all the children participating in a play activity? Do you see any children who are watching from the sidelines or wandering aimlessly around the room? Does that child need help to join a group or choose an activity? Or is she just considering what to do next? Check back in a few minutes to see if she has found something.

- *Noise:* Is there an area of the room that seems to be generating most of the noise? Why? Are voices eagerly discussing plans, or do voices sound tense? Is the equipment being misused? It may be a good idea to walk over and stand near that area and see what is going on. Sometimes the children need some help listening to each other, or sometimes just using a soft voice to help them clarify what they are doing will be enough to bring down the noise level and get them going in a better direction.
- *Individual children:* There may be a particular child who needs attention or whom you want to learn more about. What is she doing right now? What is her motivation? Do the other children like her? What can she do well? Does she have a problem at the moment? What strengths do you see in that child? What does she need to work on? Should that be an individual goal for that child?

Natural Assessment—that is, watching what children do when they are engaged in another activity, rather than following prompts from the teacher—is the most accurate way to assess young children's development and learning. When they are allowed to move freely, children will naturally use skills they have already mastered, or they will purposely practice a skill that they have *almost* mastered. Assessment opportunities during guided play include:

- *Language development:* The playhouse and the block area are great places to see language development. Are all the children using language reciprocally, or is one child directing the play? Notice what vocabulary is and is not being used. Do children know the names of objects in the area, or are they missing vocabulary? Is there a child who doesn't talk at all? How is that child participating?
- *Social skills:* The playhouse is a rich source of information, but these may also be seen in other areas of the room. In the house, are the children listening to each other and playing the same "story," or are there several different stories being played out by different children? Is there one child on the fringes of the play? Is that child observing the others, or in a world of her own? Which children strike you as needing more observation on another day? Write down their names and questions you have.
- *Empathy:* This can be seen throughout the day, especially during recess or while lining up. Which children respond kindly if someone gets hurt? Do children make room for others in a crowded space, or do they push others out of the way? Who really listens to other's ideas, and who interrupts what others are doing? These occasions can also become teaching opportunities, as teachers thank a child for his thoughtfulness, or quietly, one-on-one, suggest a friendlier way for a child to talk to other children.

- *Motor skills:* Large motor skills are best observed on the playground, especially on the climber or while learning new skills such as jumping rope, bouncing a ball, or using a hula hoop. Small motor skills can be assessed in any area of the room where children must use their hands. Teachers can add small motor activities to virtually every center in the room: puzzles and manipulatives are the obvious places, but the teacher can also put small plastic jars with screw-on lids in the dollhouse. Add small decorative pieces (such as pattern blocks) to the block area. Using adult pencils and markers in the art area is helpful for ages over 4½, as are occasional "miniature" art projects, painting with Q-tips or small watercolor brushes. Notice how the children grasp the implements and help them do it more skillfully.
- *Literacy:* Classrooms for 4-year-olds will have books available and a choice of writing or drawing implements. Other materials 4s enjoy as they begin to notice the print around them are alphabet puzzles, letter blocks for building, letter stamps, and logos cut from cereal boxes or other products familiar to children. Do some children read the names of the letters as they play with these toys? Fours can often "read" the words "STOP" or "Legos" and may like to copy the environmental print. Watch who is showing interest in letters and words, and who might be ready for the next step. While children are drawing, notice how they use their hands and whether they are choosing to write numbers and letters (don't worry if the letters and numbers are backwards at this age). In the book area notice if children are handling books correctly and also if they are "reading" them aloud to dolls or teddy bears. Children who have heard classic stories over and over will often recite what is happening as they look at the pictures. All of these are pre-literacy skills that need to be mastered before first grade.
- *Numeracy:* There are several steps in learning how to count correctly: reciting the numbers in order by rote, understanding one-to-one correspondence, and finally, to put it together and count things accurately. In the 4-year-old classroom you may see children at any of these stages, and observation during play will tell you where they are now, and what they need to learn next. If a child offers to show you a block construction, you might respond by admiring it, then saying something like: "I wonder how many rectangle blocks you used?" By watching how the child counts the blocks without your help, you will know exactly which skills are missing, if any. In the playhouse, you may observe that a child sets the table with exactly the right number of forks and cups to go with each plate, and that there is one place setting for each child. This shows that child has mastered one-to-one correspondence, even if she is not yet counting. Number puzzles will give you an opportunity to see if children can name the numerals and put them in order without teacher assistance. Or, at cleanup time you can tell one child to put away six triangle blocks and another child to put away eight square blocks. By blending numbers

and letters into the playtime, teachers can learn more about what children know without having to pull them aside for individual assessments.

Active Teacher Guidance

Through careful observation, the teacher can follow the children's evolving "play script" and understand the children's goals for their play. Any successful intervention with the children must align with the children's interests and goals. Children want to work on things that are difficult for them, but they need the calm presence of their teacher to make their play feel safe and manageable. In each of these interventions, the teacher is helping the children to have a positive experience in play together, to express their needs more clearly, to listen to and consider other people's perspectives, and to feel good about their ability to meet the teacher's expectations.

1. Environmental Adjustments

- *Two girls have been playing in the playhouse for several days in a row, following the same script. They are playing the part of babies, crawling around with pretend bottles and crying, not using language and not listening to the other children playing there. Before school the next day, the teacher adds the doctor kit to the playhouse and suggests that the babies may be crying because they are sick. Who wants to be the doctor?*
- *Teacher has noticed that play in the block area has gotten repetitive; the children seem to have run out of ideas. Before the children enter in the morning, she adds a few unusual materials to see if they will make it more interesting for the children. She does not tell them what she has done because she wants the children to begin noticing things on their own (see "extending play" below).*
- *Cleanup, especially in the dramatic play areas, has become burdensome. The teacher decides to simplify the area (remove some props) and have a clearly labeled space for each item. She also helps those children to clean up by starting them five minutes sooner and assigning specific jobs to each child.*

2. Meeting Individual Needs

- *The teacher wants to help two quiet boys who do not have many friends. She observes that one is interested in cars and the other likes to build with blocks. She sets up two trays, each with a combination of small blocks and cars on them. She uses one large block to make a bridge between the two trays. She then invites the two boys to play in this special place "just for them." Maybe they will take the bait and begin trading toys and interacting with each other, or maybe they won't. If they don't, she will let other children play there, and the next day try something different to catch their interest.*

3. Helping a Child Enter Play

A child walks into the playhouse and says something about riding on a train when everyone is playing about a pet hospital. The child entering the play is often out of alignment with the ongoing play, and he will usually be rejected by the other children saying: "You can't play here!"

- Option 1: The teacher anticipates by stopping the child, asking him to watch with her and see what the other children are playing before he tries to enter the play. After they discuss the play script, the teacher suggests a role aligned with their play: "Do you think they need an assistant doctor to help hold the animals when they get their shots?"
- Option 2: Or, the teacher might provide a prop aligned with the play for the child to offer: "Here are some blankets to keep the sick animals warm. Why don't you take them into the hospital?"
- Option 3: Or after the child seems to be getting the idea of how this works, the teacher asks the child "What do you think you can do so the children will say 'Yes, come and play?'"

Figure 3.1 Assessing a play area before entering reflects emotional intelligence
Source: Photo courtesy of Monaire Taylor.

4. Redirecting a Child (protecting others' play)

The same child wants to enter the pet hospital play, but the teacher knows this child has not developed the sophistication in thought or language to sustain and keep up with the cooperative play in progress. Not wanting to distract the other players, who are just learning about cooperative play themselves, the teacher can redirect that child in alignment with his interests.

- Option 1: *Sometimes the teacher can just stand and block the doorway, ignoring the child wanting to come in to play, as enough of a hint for the child to move along. Or she may need to point out to the child that the pet hospital looks full and offer to help her find another activity while waiting for a turn. If there is not time for the child to have a turn later, the teacher will empathize and facilitate a turn during the next play time so the child will trust her to follow through on his behalf.*
- Option 2: *The teacher might offer to show him where the trains are kept, saying, "I think I have some people in my cupboard who could ride on these trains." Offering a special toy from the cupboard can help reassure a child who is feeling a little left out.*
- Option 3: *Or, she might help him to find a playmate, saying, "Let's find someone else who wants to play trains, too. I see Suzie looking for something to do in the block area."*

5. Extending the Play with Props

Refer back to Chapter 2, "Interactive Interest Centers through the Year," for a reminder of the items that might provide new suggestions for play in an area that is no longer being well used.

6. Adding Complexity to Play

Some "Master players" are enjoying their theme of "Grandma's Coming" in the house, but the excitement is building and the play is becoming both louder and more repetitive. The teacher stops by and asks the children to tell her more about what will happen when Grandma finally gets there. She tries to draw out their own real experiences of this event with some thoughtful questions:

- "What happens after Grandma comes?"
- "Will she bring anything with her?"
- "What is her favorite food?"
- "Where will she sleep?"
- "Does she read you stories?"
- "Does she like to take the baby for a walk?"

As the teacher sees the children's interest caught by a particular question, she may bring or suggest some roles or props to support that idea:

- "Who knows how to cook her favorite food?"
- "Do you need to go to the book area to get some books for Grandma to read?"

7. Positive Redirection and Setting Limits

In their enthusiasm for experimenting with ramps and balls, some boys begin to throw some of the balls to make them go up the ramps. Pretty soon throwing the balls becomes a new game. The teacher reminds them that the balls need to stay touching the floor or the blocks (using positive speech, stating what she wants the children to do) *or may pose a more interesting problem to work out that doesn't involve throwing, by asking "I wonder what would happen if we put a basket at the end of the ramp; can you roll the balls so they go into the basket?"* (redirecting them to a related experiment).

Finally, after more observation, the teacher sees that a particular child really is only interested in throwing rather than experimenting. She quietly tells him that since it is too hard to remember to keep the balls on the ground, it is time to find a new activity. (She is clear and firm that the balls can't be thrown because it is not safe. The child who can no longer continue doing what he wants with the children he likes is reminded that he does have to listen to the teacher, and that he must manage his behavior or lose privileges.) *She may walk around the room with him a bit, calming him with her quiet presence and helping him to become interested in something else. If they can't find anything that catches his interest she may go to the cupboard and get the bean bags and a basket and set him up in a quiet spot away from others and let him throw. Although it may make the child mad to be removed from the activity, the teacher is not punishing the child but helping him find a socially acceptable activity that will meet his needs and also meet her rules for safety.*

8. Helping Children Complete and Transition

Two girls have been playing with some small blocks at the table for quite a while. The next time the teacher observes them, she sees that a number of blocks are on the floor and the girls are getting sillier by the minute, doing more giggling than building. She approaches them in a friendly way and says, "You two have been playing here for a long time. Maybe you would like to do something different. I see there's room at the art table." The girls may agree that they're done, hastily put the blocks away, and go to the art table. Or, they may protest: "No! We're not done!" If that happens, the teacher reminds them to keep the blocks on the table and walks away. Oftentimes, the girls may play for another minute or two, then decide that they really ARE done and go to the art table (the teacher's suggestion did help them recognize that they were done, but the extra time allowed them to feel that it was their decision—a win–win). *If they continue to use the blocks inappropriately, the teacher can go over and help them clean up and think of something else they would like to do. The teacher might say "I see you are really having fun playing together, but we talked about keeping the blocks on the table and they are on the floor again, so I can tell this isn't working anymore. Let's find someplace else for you two to play."*

The teacher is guiding everything that happens in the classroom. The children are allowed to use the toys as long as they use them according to his rules—and his rules include the way that they behave toward one another. True, they are freely playing and choosing what they are interested in, and choosing whom they want to play with, but the teacher manages the master plan. If the teacher is clear and consistent with his rules, and clear in his coaching for socially and emotionally constructive interactions, the classroom will run smoothly because the children will know the teacher will not let them be unkind to one another or misuse the toys or equipment. They learn to trust that the teacher will make sure they feel safe and enjoy learning together; that will make them willing learners. To summarize:

- The classroom arrangement will inform and organize the children's play.
- When ongoing small group play is under way you can manage it by adding props, removing props, adding complexity, or using positive redirection—thereby directing the play toward your goals for the children.
- Children who are unkind to another person can be told they are done but that they may come back later when they can remember to talk to others in a friendly way, just the way they like children to talk to them.
- If a child or small group runs out of ideas and the play deteriorates you can either add an idea or a prop to bring the play back to a constructive path, or you can help them transition to another activity.
- Because the children want to play, and want to be with their friends, and want to please you, you actually have a lot of power and can create a lot of the child's experience as long as the teacher's entrance into their play is aligned with what the children want to do.

Routines Supporting Guided Play

The teacher is responsible for the overall atmosphere in the classroom, as well as teaching routines that help children to take responsibility and to be more independent. Here are some examples:

1. Choosing an Activity and Beginning to Play

The teacher presents the activities which are available for that day, and calls on individual children to choose an activity. Children are dismissed to their area one at a time after they choose. The number of children allowed in a play center (particularly the playhouse and the blocks) is set by the teacher, depending on the space and materials available, and the teacher's goals for individual children. At the beginning of the year fewer children can play harmoniously together, but toward the end of the year the teacher will be able to allow larger groups and trust that they can manage. All year, he will be individualizing as well; a child who needs more time to develop social skills will do better playing with only one or two children at a time, so he will look for opportunities to set up situations where the less skilled child can practice and improve, rather than insisting on a set number of children in a certain area. If other children want to join a group that the teacher has intentionally limited, he can say matter-of-factly, "They are busy right now. You can play here later."

At centers for individual play, such as puzzles or sensory materials, the teacher considers how many children can use the area without being crowded. One helpful system is to set out exactly as many chairs or as many aprons as are needed for that number of children. The children know that if all the chairs are taken or all the aprons are in use that that area is full for now. But here, too, the teacher can be flexible; if two children ask to work together on a difficult puzzle, they should be allowed to try it.

In a large group of children, it is easy for those who listen quietly and follow directions to get lost in the shuffle. One way to be sure that everyone gets a turn to choose first is to assign a day of the week to each child, so on Monday the "Monday children" can choose first, then the "Tuesday children" go first on Tuesdays, etc. If you have enough centers available, everyone will have at least one day when they get their first choice.

2. Changing from One Activity to Another

When children want to move to a different activity, they know (because the teacher has taught them) how to put away the toys they were using before they go to a different area. Again, they can only enter a new activity if there are space and materials for them to play there. In the case of cooperative play (in the house or the blocks) they will need to ask the children who are already there if they can join in. If the children say, "yes," they enter and begin to play. If the children say, "no," they will go and look for something else to do. (The teacher has also taught the children polite ways to say "no," such as "Not now. You can play with us next time.") It may help to enter play with an idea to enhance what is already going on. For example, "Oh, your baby is sick? I'll be the doctor." The teacher can suggest a role like this to a child who is ready to enter the play but may not have very good strategies to do so. This avoids power plays by children who love having the power to say "no."

3. Cleaning Up

Every good teacher is occasionally tempted to simplify activities, or eliminate art materials, so that it will be easier to clean up. The antidote to this temptation is teaching strong cleanup procedures, and helping the children understand that part of being "good classroom citizens" is cleaning up and leaving things nice for the next children who will use them. This is another lifelong concept and attitude the children are learning—important not just for the harmony in this classroom but, more importantly, for harmony in all their future classrooms, homes, places of work, and interpersonal relationships. Cleanup also provides a good sense of completion, an important step in any activity.

If a child decides to leave a cooperative play group, the teacher can help by asking the other children if there is something they are no longer using, so that child can put it away. Such a token clean up reinforces the idea that they are "done" playing there, and excuses them from cleaning up there at the general cleanup time.

Several minutes before the general clean up, the teacher will quietly go to any areas that are more complicated to clean up (perhaps blocks or painting) and ask those children to start cleaning up early. Ideally, the teacher already gave them a five-minute warning that soon it would be time to dismantle their buildings or finish their pictures. This is all done quietly so that other groups can continue their play for a while longer without interruption. (See also "Transitions," following in this chapter.)

Meeting Developmental Goals through Facilitated Play

1. Clarifying the Play

As the teacher observes the play she may notice, especially with younger children, that the players have not been communicating their intentions to each other, and may be headed on a collision course. It can be helpful to suggest that a child move over, for example, if two block structures are too close together, or someone's elbow keeps interfering with another child's toys. Providing sufficient space and clear boundaries for each child helps avoid future problems.

In dramatic play, the teacher can help guide children toward greater cooperation by asking questions. Each child may have a different idea of what is going on. Open-ended questions such as: "What game are you playing?" or "Who is the mother?" or "Are you all building the same building, or are you next door neighbors?" help children to say out loud what they have been thinking, and will alert the other children to what is going on around them. Sometimes the teacher may stay to facilitate a conversation until the children have come to an agreement about what the ground rules are.

2. Increasing Children's Attention Span

Children increase their persistence and engagement in play gradually with practice. The teacher can help by observing the play and looking for opportunities to extend their ideas or add complexity to what they are doing. This is especially true in

Figure 3.2 The teacher may need to help these girls find a focus for their play
Source: Photo courtesy of Geraldine Rocha.

dramatic play and block building. Both areas should have some "add to" toys close at hand for the teacher to bring out when he notices the children seem to be losing interest. For example, a doctor's kit may extend house play into doctor play. The teacher who hears a child say, "My baby is sick," might just quietly pull the doctor's kit from the nearby cupboard and set it on the shelf. When the teacher's suggestions are in harmony with what the children are already thinking and playing about, the props will probably be welcomed and quickly incorporated into the play.

Add-to toys for the blocks should include cars, animals (farm or zoo), and people, all to the same scale as the blocks. Some teachers make a rule that the children need to build something first, then add the toys. Others let them begin playing with the animals, for example, then ask, "Where do the animals sleep?" "Do they need a house or a cage?" "What do they eat?" "What can we use for pretend food?" etc.

Open-ended questions can lead the play into new directions. Another example is when some children have been driving little cars around and around on a road made of blocks, but that game is beginning to get repetitious. The teacher might ask, "What else do your cars need? Where do they go to get gas? What if they break down? Is there a repair shop?" etc. These ideas may send the children back to the block shelf to build more things for their cars.

3. Helping Children Know When to Stop

Learning how to stop when a game has become repetitive or boring is a skill that also takes practice. A teacher may notice that three friends have been playing together for some time and enjoying each other's company. After a while they become very silly, acting much younger than their age and laughing at the same jokes over and over. Rather than wait until someone ends up crying or misusing materials, the teacher decides to intervene. "You have been playing here for a long time, and I can see you're getting finished with it. I'll help you clean this up, and look for another place to play." If they protest, he might suggest another activity, name what he is seeing ("I see you're not really playing store anymore, you're just saying silly things to each other") or say, "Well, I'll be back in a few minutes, and then we can think about going to see the new colors I put in the art area today," or something similar. About two minutes later, he will come back and say, "Now it's time to put these away, and I'll help you find something else to do. I see that the Lego table is empty."

Monitoring the Ambience in the Room

1. Noise Level and Energy Level

Playtime is never very quiet, but the teacher should aim for a "busy hum" of activity, rather like that of a beehive. Children talking together in friendly voices; the click of blocks on the rug; girls giggling at a secret joke in the house; someone humming softly as he paints, chairs sliding in and out from tables; and an occasional "I did it!" from the puzzle table. Of course, lots of rugs, curtains, and acoustic tiles are helpful, but even a hard-surfaced room is more pleasant to listen to when children are engaged in constructive play.

The teacher's voice is the most powerful tool for cultivating soft voices among the children. If the teacher makes it a point to come close to the children and speak to them in a soft voice children will respond in kind. The teacher who yells across the room to someone should not be surprised when the children yell too.

Other things to monitor are the temperature, type and amount of light, and general ambience of the classroom. A room that is too hot or too bright can cause people to feel irritable. Alternatively, a fish tank or some growing plants will have a calming effect on everyone.

When the teacher hears the energy level rising in a particular group or child, his calm presence in proximity to that child (or children) will have a grounding effect. Sensory motor activities (playdough, sand, water) can also help the over-excited or crying child to calm and re-center. Bright colors in the art center provide another way for children to express their strong feelings in a positive way.

2. Play-Alone Spaces

Sometimes a child just needs time apart from the group; it requires a lot of emotional energy and higher-level skills to compromise and get along with others. Perhaps the day started badly, or it could just be that the child wants some time alone. It's good to have a small table and chair off in a quiet corner somewhere that is just right for one child to play alone with a special toy. Play-alone toys are little sets of things that go together in different ways, but just enough for one child. It may be some small table blocks and a few miniature animals or people, or a special set of glitter crayons and fancy paper to draw on. Or it might be a place at the sink with some soapy water, a rubber doll, and a washcloth. It's a good idea to have a few different play-alone toy sets in a cupboard to be taken out when the need arises.

Other children can be told (if they ask) that Sam wants to play by himself for a while. This sends everyone the message that the teacher takes care of the needs of all the children, and they can be sure that he will take care of them, too, if they need some extra help. The play-alone space is available to anyone who wants a little time away from the group. Children learn that if it is too much work to play socially, it is a perfectly acceptable strategy to retreat, regroup, and try again later.

3. Keeping It Interesting

Most of the "ambience" in the classroom comes from the children's whole-hearted involvement in their play. When the children are not playing well, nothing works. The first thing the teacher does when he notices that the play is not sparking the children's curiosity, creativity, or delight in new discoveries, is to look at the environment. Have the same old toys been there since September? Are some toys so difficult they produce frustration? Or are they so simple they invite silliness and boredom? Are spaces too crowded? Shelves in disarray? Puzzle pieces missing?

Fortunately, it does not require a million different toys to keep children interested. The beauty of open-ended toys like blocks and art materials is that the children will make their play harder for themselves as they master the easy things. First they will stack blocks and line them up, then they will cover the floor with them, then they will make walls for buildings, then they will make taller and harder walls with roofs, then they will make elaborate balancing sculptures. Small changes every few weeks in these areas will bring the children back to something they thought they were finished with, and the play will start up again with more complexity. By making these changes when the children are gone, the teacher creates regular opportunities for the children to "discover" something new and interesting in the different play areas.

- Put cupcake papers or pieces of curly ribbon in the art area. What will the children think to make with them?

- Stow away puzzles no one is interested in and put a tray of frozen peas or canned beans and toothpicks out instead as a new construction toy.
- How about a pack of baseball cards? What conversations will that stimulate? Can a group of baseball fans figure out a way to share the cards among themselves? What game will they invent with them?
- Add food coloring to the water table.
- Put some odd-shaped blocks or crosswise slices of a tree branch on the block shelf.
- Wrap an empty box like a present, and put it in the playhouse.
- Find some library books with big color pictures of garden pests to put in the science center.
- Use your imagination! If you are having fun spicing up the centers, the children will have fun, too. You will also be inspired as you watch themes develop, thinking "These children are so interested in playing 'going to work'—I'll bring in some old purses that will serve as briefcases." Keep your changes small, and space them out over the year, one or two at a time. That way the children will always be a bit surprised, and you won't run out of ideas.

Figure 3.3 Individualized teaching
Source: Photo courtesy of Monaire Taylor.

Anxiety

The teacher notices a boy who tends to get silly as lunch is drawing to a close, and that it continues as the group returns to the classroom which then creates challenges during storytime. Before lunch is over the teacher stands near the boy with a sponge, and asks him to wipe down the table while the class lines up to leave the cafeteria. When the child finishes washing the table off the teacher brings him to the front of the line to walk with him and ask him to help pass out the rest mats. The teacher has realized that the silly behavior is a sign of his anxiety about being unsure about whether he can manage what comes next. By giving the child focused jobs and telling him what to do, the teacher eliminates the problem.

Undeveloped Skills

The teacher sees that Jake accidentally bumps down the other children's blocks nearly every time he plays there; it seems unintentional, but happens whenever he is carrying blocks and toys to his building. Jake says he is sorry and tries to help repair the damage. Reflecting, the teacher realizes that Jake also has a difficult time using the latch on the bathroom door, that his jacket is one of the jackets that never stays on its hook, and that he has shown no interest in the art and drawing table. Wondering if he has trouble with his small muscle control, he sets out several activities in the yard and classroom to encourage Jake to use his hands and his pincer grasp, so the teacher can observe more. He sets out clothes pins in a bowl with a narrow lip and a pattern paper showing a pattern of red, yellow and blue clips going around the edge of the thin plastic bowl. The teacher demonstrates the "new toy." He shows the children that they can play a game by rolling a die, counting the dots of the die, and clipping that number of clothes pins to the edge of the bowl. Announcing that two children can use this toy he chooses Jake's best friend to be the first one to play with the new toy, and suggests he pick a friend to join him.

In the yard, the teacher stuffs several light plastic grocery bags with crumpled newspaper and hangs them up on the chain link fence high above the children's reach. He draws a circle on the bag with permanent marker and sets out three squirt bottles with colored water. When he tells the children about the new activity in the yard, he suggests that children squirt at the target and see if they can move the bag. He puts out playdough with plastic knives and extruders, and tongs with a basket of cotton balls and an ice tray to sort them into. He also puts out sidewalk chalk in the yard, hoping he can inspire some writing. When it is time to go to the yard, the teacher dismisses Jake first, hoping that he will choose one of these activities designed to build his hand strength and fine motor dexterity.

The teacher sees that Jake has to concentrate very hard when he tries to coordinate his hands to pursue various activities, and often ends up grasping with his entire hand rather than individual fingers; no wonder he is dropping things and not interested in writing. At the playdough table the teacher suggested Jake pinch the playdough; Jake did it for a brief time but quickly tired of it. Each day the teacher will be setting out toys to stimulate his use of his hands—this is individualizing the curriculum for Jake without needing to call out "special needs." Of course any child will enjoy and get something from using the toys set out for Jake. That is the beauty of playtime; no one is particularly singled out to be helped, but all around the classroom this teacher is being very intentional about what he is putting out to meet both the needs of the group and the needs of individual children. As time goes by the teacher will evaluate Jake's progress and consider whether he needs to be referred for occupational therapy.

Jake is not the only child he is planning for; Sally talks so loud and so fast that the children don't listen to her—in fact, they walk away when she approaches them. All day, he's watching for opportunities to say quietly to her "Remember, tell them quietly so they will listen." Soon he will only need to catch her eye and she will lower her voice and slow down. When it is playtime Bubba goes to the drinking fountain and watches the children, quickly turning to take a drink whenever anyone approaches the fountain. The teacher puts plastic frogs and floats some bark in a tub of water, and sets it with an apron on the shelf next to the drinking fountain. This new activity draws other children to Bubba and offers him something to do with water. This individualizing of the curriculum facilitates the children's play in the beginning of the year; by the middle of the year the teacher will be extending the play. Perhaps he will put another tub by the first, adding a plastic pollywog so there can be a frog family. Along with the frogs, bark, and some rocks he also adds a log so that the frogs can hop from one tub to the other tub … as the frogs make friends, so will the children.

Themes that Reflect Development

Every teacher sees interests evolve over the course of the year. Themes that emerge in play provide clues about the children's brain development; they provide insight to what they are thinking about and working to understand. Many of these symbolic games repeat year after year, as every child this age who has an opportunity to play through his learning and changing perspective will touch on these topics. Some perennially popular themes among 4- and 5-year-old children are:

- Games of trying to avoid "hot lava" and/or "quicksand"—both of these ideas symbolize the big, scary, uncontrollable world that could swallow you up, and a world which you must learn to maneuver through. Acting out how hard and scary it is to navigate these challenges reduces the child's anxiety when he is really asked to manage the bigger world.
- Rescuing games, princesses, victims, and babies; themes around power and control are very strong among these young children as they work on issues regarding who is in control of them and who they control. It is common to see games in which someone vulnerable needs to be protected, and with scaffolding teachers can strengthen the child's internal story by introducing empowerment into their play.

- Superhero play, managing and being bad guys and good guys; all represent the questions they have about who is in charge. Who has the power and who is in control are all very present in the children's lively minds and their play.

Seeing the play as a way in to help the children understand their world and manage their behavior gives the teacher opportunities to help develop the child's understanding of himself and his world, which in turn gives the child more control over his own behavior. There will also be the occasional theme inspired by things happening in the world, or a student's insatiable interest like the Olympic Games or saving the whales. Group themes bring the class together and strengthen community, and curriculum can easily be interwoven through the children's interests, while at the same time supporting every child's individual needs. (See Emergent Curriculum in Chapter 6.)

Infusing Play with Literacy and Numeracy

As the year progresses transitional classrooms begin to include more academics, although this will look different in different age groups. All 4- and 5-year-olds still benefit from constructive play that is guided by a skilled teacher, and their time for that kind of play needs to be protected. In fact, playtime can be expanded, as children increase their stamina, invent more sophisticated scenarios, and even integrate some academic skills into their play—with the teacher's help.

Figure 3.4 Older children can play simple games involving counting
Source: Photo courtesy of Monaire Taylor.

While the teacher is observing, assessing, and guiding the play, she may also notice opportunities to suggest extensions that involve using letters, words, and numbers. As with other extensions to play that the teacher may suggest (such as building a gas station for the cars in the block area, or taking a doll on a picnic) her suggestions are just that—only suggestions, as she wants to leave the play in the children's hands. However, if she has been observing closely, she will notice what the children are interested in, and they will welcome her suggestions because they fit into the theme of the play. When the children do not seem interested, it is best just to let that idea go. Maybe they will try it on another day.

One advantage of linking literacy to play is that children are intensely interested in what they have been imagining, and therefore are very motivated to extend their ideas into print. Here are some ideas for reading and writing extensions that work well with play, arranged from basic to more sophisticated:

- *Dictation*: The earliest form of exposing children to print is to take dictation from them about their own artwork—even scribbles! After the picture is completed, the teacher says, "Tell me about your picture," and writes down exactly what the child says, and reads it back to the child. If there is another adult in the room, the teacher may suggest the child take it to that person to read it to them. This can be an eye-opener for children who have limited experience with print. ("How did you know what I said?")
- *Writing names*: Younger children may just be learning to write their names on their artwork, so teachers can provide name cards for them to copy, or may lightly print the child's name on their work so children can trace over it if they like. (This should not be "required" if it will discourage children from doing art.)
- *Labeling block structures*: This is best suggested after the building has been completed and the teacher is invited to admire their work. After suitable admiring, the teacher might say, "Do you need a sign that says, 'gas station' so the cars know where to find it?" If the children agree, then the teacher writes the words on a card for the children to copy, and provides tape for them to tape it to their structure. The sign may be misspelled and have letters reversed at first, but this is an important step in teaching children that print has meaning and provides useful information.
- *Labeling areas in dramatic play*: This can be suggested while the children are still playing, or deciding where things are happening. They may like a sign that says "Doctor" or "Office" or "Restaurant" to go with the game they are playing. They copy the sign and the teacher helps them find a place to hang it.
- In more sophisticated group play, children may create a puppet show or a dance performance that they want to invite their friends to see. Not only can they make a sign announcing the show, but they can also provide a sign-in sheet on a clipboard for the audience to "sign in" as they arrive or cut paper into tickets which can be handed out to children and collected as they come to the show.

- Adding props to the dramatic play area is another way to inspire older Kindergarteners to include writing in their scenarios. For example, newspaper ads from a grocery store may be paired with a clipboard and paper to make a shopping list (copying words from the ads). Or a teacher can create some simple menus at the "restaurant" with pictures and names of favorite food and prices. The waiter may copy words or use his own scribbles to write down what food has been ordered.
- Wooden puzzles of the alphabet come in all shapes and sizes. Choose puzzles with larger pieces for 4s and smaller ones for 5s. If you have several different puzzles, they can be changed periodically, to keep up interest. After they have put the puzzle together, they may point to the letters as they sing the Alphabet Song, or the teacher might point to random letters to see how many the child knows. Another activity is to find the letters in one's name and spell them out to a friend.
- Literacy is more than learning letters and sounds. It is also the ability to enjoy and retell favorite stories. Felt board versions of well-known stories are a great resource. During storytime the teacher can model how the story is told, while moving the felt figures around the board. Gradually release responsibility to the children by letting them help tell the story and move the figures on the board. After a week or two of practice, leave the felt board and figures accessible to them and offer it as an interest center during play. This is a good activity for two to play together, as they take turns telling and listening to the story.

Figure 3.5 Discreet labels offer literacy without clutter
Source: Photo courtesy of Geraldine Rocha.

- A little later in the year, add a "Literacy Center" as an interest center during playtime. Older 4s and Kindergarteners enjoy copying high interest words, especially if they are related to a classroom theme or a holiday. Provide picture/word cards and different kinds of writing materials, and different colors or shapes of paper for them to write on. As the year goes on, the teacher may add tracing paper, stationery and envelopes, and name cards of all the students in the class, along with their pictures. There may also be a "mailbox" somewhere nearby, or children may put their letters in a friend's cubby.
- Kindergarteners enjoy making their own little books. Provide small blank books by folding and stapling half-sheets of paper, and word/picture cards that children can copy. They can copy the pictures (or draw their own) and words, then "read" their books to the teacher, other children, and their parents.
- For older 5s and 6-year-olds nearing the end of Kindergarten, the teacher may extend the play further by helping the whole class (after the playing is done) to dictate a language experience story about what they were pretending. These stories can be chorally read by the whole class with teacher support, and left posted at the children's eye level so children can choose to "read" them with the teacher's pointer during another free choice time.

Numeracy—as well as other math concepts—can also be woven into play. Here are some examples:

- Counting along with the teacher or a friend is one of the first steps. "How many cars does your train have?" or "I wonder how many triangle blocks you used to make this fence?" is fun to do, as long as it is timed not to interrupt the play.
- On the back of name cards, the teacher might add birthdays for children to copy.
- Puzzles with numbers or shapes on them are also good for all ages. Provide puzzles of different levels of difficulty to last through the year.
- Incorporate play money into dramatic play, which might be paying bus or train fare, buying groceries at the classroom store, or paying to see a puppet show. The teacher can reinforce particular goals she has by varying the money that is available. Perhaps she would like to use only paper currency, so children can learn to read the numerals on the bills; or perhaps she wants to use only coins so Kindergarteners can learn to recognize dimes, pennies, and nickels.
- Teacher-created materials can be added to the puzzle table. Self-checking materials work best, because the child can learn even when the teacher is not there to help. Think of a matching game with dots and numerals that only fit together when done the right way, for example.
- A deck of cards can be sorted in many different ways: matching the numerals, matching the suits, or simply dealing the same number of cards to each friend,

then counting to see if everyone has the same amount. This works better if the teacher first demonstrates the different ways that cards can be used.
- Develop a "Math Center" that might include a balance scale and blocks of the same size, for children to practice making it balance; sorting trays (or egg cartons) and small items that can be sorted in different ways: buttons or small items with different colors and shapes; stacking or nesting toys that have to fit together; number cards to put in order; pattern blocks and simple ABAB patterns for children to match or copy. Although these materials are "academic" the ingredient that makes them "playful" is that children are free to choose which ones interest them, and to use the materials in non-math ways. If a child wants to make a picture with the pattern blocks, instead of making ABAB patterns, that is all part of the process.

Young children are learning everything about everything all of the time. Play is one way that they understand the world around them. A visit to the doctor's office for a shot might have been scary—but playing it over and over in a safe environment can help children master their fear. After that, they may continue to play doctor as a fun way to interact with their friends, and the teacher might teach them what the instruments are called: "hypodermic," "blood pressure cuff," and "stethoscope" are fun words to learn how to say.

The same is true of letters, numbers, and academic language: by incorporating these symbols into play, the teacher connects them to the children's lives outside of school, and makes academic learning come alive.

Creating Smooth Transitions

Helping young children to move as a group from one activity to another can be difficult because:

- Young children have difficulty stopping and starting activities in general.
- Young children move at their own pace, so they are not all finished with their activities at the same time; nor are they all ready to begin a new activity at the same time.
- Young children are interested in many things (what the other children are doing, interesting displays in the classroom, or how they are feeling in the moment). Their inner agenda may not be the same as the teacher's agenda for what should happen next.
- Young children are physically active, and not good at waiting—whether it is standing in line or sitting quietly on the rug or in their chairs.

Thinking through a smooth transition from one activity to the next both helps your classroom be a more pleasant place and also shows the teacher's respect for the children's developmental needs. As 4s, 5s, and 6s become more independent and skillful, they like to do things for themselves at their own pace. Handling themselves independently builds self-confidence and enhances their self-esteem; the belief that "I can take care of myself" is a hallmark of maturity. Rushing a child through a transition causes anxiety and diminishes the child's feeling of mastery. Often adults forget how long it takes a 4-year-old to find the zipper on his jacket, or how worried a 5-year-old might feel if everyone is waiting for her to find her lunch.

In planning a gradual and orderly transition from one activity to another the teacher thinks through all the necessary steps, and includes a plan for children who need to wait for the rest of the group.

One of the most difficult transitions in the classroom is when it is time for the children to clean up from play and come back to their seats for a teacher-led activity. Allowing children to move at their own pace, when they are ready, will make the process more pleasant (see Cleaning Up in The Teacher's Role in Guiding Play). Since not everyone will finish putting away toys at the same time, there needs to be a "transitional activity" for children to do while waiting for others to finish. However, the teacher finesses this process by planning how much time each group may need to clean up and who is ready to begin. The goal is for every child to feel his time is well used, not spent waiting with nothing to do (remember the PreK program with disappointing outcomes mentioned in Chapter 1, where the children spent 27 percent of their day waiting for something). Not only does that waste the child's time, but also idle time is when a busy, creative mind can get in trouble while trying to amuse itself!

Here is a sample step-by-step routine for cleaning up an entire, busy play-based classroom that can be adapted to work in most transitional classrooms.

Setting the Stage for a Transition

First, the teacher decides when to begin the transition, based on how well the children are playing, how engaged they are in their explorations, and what needs to happen next in the day. The time spent on guided play can vary, becoming longer as the children mature, or even changing from day to day based on the energy and mood of the group. It's good to have some flexibility to allow time to finish the play when children are ready for a new activity. If there is a fixed time limit, the teacher can still decide how much cleanup time the children will need on this day, and when to begin the process.

The transition will be gradual, to allow children who are very engaged in play to disengage gradually, while allowing children who are ready to move on to do so quickly. The teacher will quietly speak to each group of children rather than make a general signal to the class which will distract those who are well-engaged. Her goal is that some will continue playing while others begin putting away their toys.

A planned and taught "transitional activity" will give those who finish early something to do while they wait for others to finish up and join them. Teaching and practicing the transitional activity with the whole class, the way you would teach any routine, is the first step. It should be an activity that is both independent and engaging. Some activities that work are: sitting and looking at books, singing along with a CD of favorite songs, or helping other children who have more cleaning up to do.

Orchestrating the Transition

- Before beginning the transition, the teacher gathers the materials for the next activity/lesson so that those children will not have additional "wait time" once they are done. (Or do this before playtime begins, if possible.)
- The teacher decides which group of children should clean up first, and approaches them quietly—so that other children can continue with their play. Many times the teacher will choose children who are not very engaged in their play and are ready for a change. On other days the teacher will first choose an area where children are deeply engaged, knowing that it will take the most time (such as an elaborate block building or a complex art project). If the block-builders or artists are still very engaged, the teacher will begin by giving them a five-minute warning so they can finish up and begin to think about changing activities. Try to make sure that "five-minute warnings" really are five minutes, so children begin to get a feel for how long that is. Use a timer to keep track. If a group needs more time, follow the five minutes with one extra minute of grace. Too many "warnings" become meaningless.
- The teacher can help with difficult cleanup. In general, play areas should be set up simply, so that the children will know where everything goes and can handle cleanup independently. But sometimes the play has become so elaborate (which is a good thing!) that the players will need some help organizing their cleanup. The teacher can help them by assigning specific jobs to each child, or by handing the children toys to put on the shelves. This should be done before the rest of the class begins to clean up. After the children in that area are involved in cleaning up independently, the teacher can move to the next group.
- The teacher moves strategically from one group to the next, deciding who is ready and who needs more time. She quietly approaches each group separately and can give a one-minute warning to children who are almost ready for a change. Some children will notice when others are cleaning up and begin to clean up on their own. That means they were ready for a change; those deeply engaged in their play will not even notice what others are doing.
- The teacher keeps an eye on children who are done, reinforcing the routines children have learned for the transitional activity. "Jonah is turning the pages

of his book so carefully" or "Your singing is so nice to hear!" remind them that the teacher knows they are there and notices their cooperation. Most days the children only have to wait about five to seven minutes for the rest of the class to finish. If one child is unable to stay engaged on the rug or at his seat, the teacher might assign him a job to help with cleanup.

Most children do not like to miss out on what their friends are doing, so if just one or two children are dawdling with cleanup, begin the next activity with the rest of the class. The stragglers will usually finish right up so they can join the group.

Creating and Adapting Transitions

Because every situation is a bit different, teachers will need to think up their own gradual transitions in their day. What will be the routine for passing out papers, getting backpacks and lining up to go home? What can children do while standing in line before the lunch bell rings? How do children come in from recess—do they know where to go next?

First, imagine how the transition will feel from the point of view of one child: What can I do while I'm waiting for my turn? What are the steps I will need to remember? Where do I go next? What should I do when I get there? These are the steps to teach and practice with the children.

Then, imagine the way you would like the routine to happen. What will be the steps? How will one step lead smoothly to the next step? Will there be a visual cue for each step, or will the child just have to remember what's next?

Are there any spots where children will be too crowded? (For example, how many children can use the coat rack at one time? Is there a better place to put the pencil boxes so they can be more spread out?) How many children can I send to get their things at once?

Will the children have to wait at their seats? What can they do? Putting a box of picture books on each table will give the "waiters" something to do for a few minutes. Some teachers play a CD or sing a song while the transition is in progress, and the children can join in.

Is this transition too complicated? How might it be simplified and streamlined? After you have tried it with your class and identified any bottlenecks or difficult steps for the children, you might make adjustments.

You will teach this routine the way you would teach any new routine, monitoring and giving reminders until all the children are able to do it on their own. Occasionally observing how things are going and praising those children who are managing well reinforces good habits. Remember that routines and transitions are not made of stone. As the children grow and their bodies take up more space, their abilities to handle themselves will improve. A transition that used to work well may need tweaking later in the year. If you decide to change a routine, that change also needs to be explicitly taught to avoid confusion. Explaining the reason for any changes to the process is an excellent opportunity for them to see flexible thinking, problem-solving, and how to change something that is not working the way you envisioned it.

Specific Play Areas in the Classroom

Dramatic Play

Children use dramatic play to practice and "think through" the experiences they don't understand in their everyday lives. They practice what it might be like to be mommy or daddy, and as they play these parts they build empathy for adult roles and responsibilities. The teacher's goal for children involved in dramatic play is to help them use language, extend their attention spans, be creative in their thinking and problem-solving, and learn that they can successfully manage their behavior and impulses in social situations. Supervising dramatic play areas during guided play is often about helping children problem-solve and better understand how to get along with each other. While the playhouse is an obvious venue for dramatic play, the block area also often includes dramatic play as children build socially based structures like houses, schools or offices and play out stories within them. In early dramatic play children need the props and supports of a playhouse to give them ideas; as they develop more abstract thought they can move it into small spaces where dollhouse people (or even something like clothespins!) can represent the people whose roles they are playing.

Playhouse

This activity is very self-directed, but teachers may need to help children stay focused on their play, and offer ideas or materials to keep the play constructive or extend their play. Children should become "lost in their play," exploring and experimenting with the roles they take on, and so deep in their imaginations that they lose touch with what is going on in other areas of the classroom. The teacher may be needed to help children avoid getting too silly or excited in the joy of play, causing the play to devolve. Help keep the play on track by putting toys away that are not being used; not only will lots of toys be a daunting task at cleanup, but the clutter also clutters the child's thinking and keeps the play from progressing in a purposeful way. It can also help children to have the teacher stop by and ask about the story they are playing; if she sees a child dumping all the dishes onto the floor she might suggest a constructive play scenario that incorporates that: "Oh no, did all the dishes drop when you were cooking dinner? You'd better tell your guests that they'll have to wait for you to pick up and get the spaghetti cooking on the stove! Here, let me help—you start the spaghetti and I'll put the dishes on the table." At this point the child may have received the suggestion he needed to keep playing, or he may decide he would rather go stir sand around in the sensory table.

One of the teacher's jobs is to protect children who are playing well from interruptions by other children; the dynamics of the play need to be respected in these social situations. If children want to join the play they need to ask, and the answer needs to be respected. If the children do not want anyone to join them, the teacher needs to help the other child understand that it's not personal, but just means that those two or three are busy. Remember that playing with one other child is easier than playing with two other children. It can be challenging to young children to speak up for their needs, and to listen to another child's wants and needs and work it out so things feel fair and fun. Adding a third child increases the number of issues the child needs to keep in her mind while being social. (Four children are generally easier than three as the foursome usually splits into two pairs of two players.)

Sometimes the children playing could include another but they don't quite know how to do it; if the teacher has a feel for this it is best not to suggest that a child ask "Can I play?" Here the teacher may make a helpful suggestion, based on observation of the developing play, which creates an entrance for another child: "Susie, would you like to see if they need a babysitter for the baby while they go out to the store?" Or, if the teacher has a small toolbox in the cupboard she can give it to Susie with the suggestion that she knock on the door and tell the others she needs to fix the leak under the sink.

Awareness of the children's stage of play will ensure that your guidance will mesh with what they can do. Young 4-year-olds, or immature older 4s, often are very happy with everyone being the mom or a family of big sisters while baby drinks from the catsup bottle; each is following his or her own agenda for play and there is no concern that it does not make cohesive sense. This is known as "Associative" play: children are getting along pretty well in the space, but they are each following their own ideas without needing to negotiate; if there is a conflict in goals it is likely one child will leave the play. More mature players who are interested in a group theme will have other ideas about the roles so that they fit into a whole—"No, there's already a baby but we need a grandma to babysit." The wise teacher looks through the lens of development and waits and watches to get her clues from the children's play before stepping in. The children really need help figuring out how to get along, be friends, and stay in relationships with each other more than anything else. Coaching and clarification of confusions is an important part of the teacher's role while children use the dollhouse.

When children are turning 5 and have had some experience playing in the house, they may be ready to make the play more cooperative with a group agreement about the play theme, each person's role, and sticking with that character. In true "Cooperative Play" the children are more interested in being part of the group creating themes, plots, and roles together than they are in getting their own way. When adults reflect on play with other children this is often the kind of play they remember, around the age of 5—some regular gathering of friends or cousins where the group of children swooped as a flock from one idea to another. To encourage more cooperation, the teacher can ask each child to tell her what the play is about and the roles they are playing: "Who are you? Oh, you're the waiter in the restaurant. Is the restaurant on fire? Is that why Nan has the fire hose?" Naming the role aloud in front of others helps the children to understand what is going on in each other's minds, and helps make the game more cohesive. Another way to encourage cooperation at this stage is to reduce the number of duplicate props (only one baby doll, instead of three or four) so they can decide who is the mother, the father or other mother, the big brother, the babysitter, etc. Negotiating and compromising on the roles shows that the children are truly cooperating, because keeping the play going is now more important than getting one's own way.

Small Unit Blocks

Unit blocks are made of hardwood so they will outlast generations of children, and they are classic, wonderful teaching toys when they are used with care. They support many pre-math concepts as children compare size, shape, and balance while they build. Some helpful rules that keep the blocks safe: blocks must be lifted, moved and put in place carefully with one's hands (not thrown, knocked over, walked on or kicked). Children playing in the block area need to pay attention to their bodies so that others' work will not be inadvertently disturbed. Young children who begin taking blocks off the shelf may find that activity in itself so satisfying that they need to be reminded to use the blocks for a project. You can ask them what they are planning to make—not because it matters what they make, but to focus their attention on the building aspect rather than just piling them on the floor.

If young children seem to need ideas about how to use the blocks, the teacher may model some simple construction such as by making enclosed spaces ("buildings" in which one might place cars, farm animals, etc.) and roads. As the children get older and more experienced the construction can become very creative and artistic, taking on the feeling of sculpture. Children playing in this area with strong ideas may need protection from other children wanting to join in and interfere with the creative process, or they may need help from the teacher to clarify their plans for other children who are playing with them. By placing blocks in a corner, with the block shelf forming a third wall, it is easy for the teacher to manage the flow of children in and out. Teachers pay close attention to this play to support friendships as twosomes work together, and to protect the process and anticipate completion of the play which may need her facilitation.

Figure 3.6 Unit blocks and props offer unlimited options for play
Source: Photo courtesy of Geraldine Rocha.

Good teachers always want play to end on a positive note so the children will want to come back to try again. Children who are not yet adept at recognizing that they have played out their ideas and are ready to move on may knock blocks over because they do not know how to acknowledge that they are finished and begin cleaning up. Helping children finish up and move on to the next activity by stopping before they run out of ideas or get excited and silly helps them complete play on a positive note.

Children may need help cleaning up, as this play consumes a lot of thought and energy. The teacher frames cleaning up as the pleasure of taking care of things you love and enjoy and want others to enjoy as well, not as a punishment for having used them. Help the children break the task down to manageable work (one child puts the triangle blocks away and another puts the cars away); putting away a big pile of blocks can feel overwhelming so expect to help the children as they learn and demonstrate the need for adult help. It is easy to teach math skills and vocabulary as the children sort the blocks by sizes and shapes while putting them away.

Extending block play with cars and trucks, plastic farm animals, small plastic people and small dollhouse furniture, can keep children busy for long periods of time. Adding small objects to put in trucks, and even colored blocks to add to natural wood blocks for design elements will extend the blocks again. Natural objects such as pieces of driftwood, or rounds of wood cut in posts or "cookies" all extend play.

Art in the Child-Initiated Classroom

The Value of Open-Ended Art in the Curriculum

- *Art draws on the right side of the brain.* Thinking visually builds a different, equally important, area of the brain than does language or logic.
- *Art creates beauty and builds self-esteem.* The design created by forms, lines, dots, and the juxtaposition of different colors is always interesting to the child, and sometimes beautiful as well. The act of finding and creating beauty from the void is centering and calming. The fact that "I made that!" is empowering to young children.
- *Art develops an eye for patterns and design.* Seeing similarities, differences, relationships and sequences are all part of expanding the brain.
- *Art develops motor skills and self-regulation.* Controlling a crayon, a large easel brush or a small watercolor brush, all require different hand and arm muscles. Making that small dot of glue from a bottle requires not only muscle strength to squeeze the bottle, but also self-regulation to STOP squeezing the bottle.
- *Art provides a constructive means of emotional expression.* Young children often do not have the words to express their feelings, whether positive or negative. The process of painting, drawing, or even scribbling about their feelings helps children to release them in a positive way. Sometimes creating art about strong feelings provides a venue for children to talk about them with an adult.
- *Art communicates as no words can.* On the first day back after a traumatic injury, Josh painted a picture of his newly broken arm over the entire 18" by 24" easel paper with black and brown and faint swirls of red. He finished the picture with a tiny splash of neon green right in the center of the picture. "That's where the hurt is," he commented. Food-conscious Anabel painted a self-portrait of a not-too-happy child with her birthday cake beside her and "a little bit of cheddar," an orange splot in her hand.
- *Art helps children give meaning to confusing events.* When words do not suffice, visual art can help children to organize and better understand events in their lives. This understanding—while the child is in control of the crayon or the brush—helps the child to gain mastery over her feelings of confusion or anxiety generated by events that she was not equipped to understand.

Art is fun! The gooshy feel of finger paint, the running together of colors in a watercolor, the surprise of creating something unexpected out of paper and glue—all these are rewards in themselves that draw the child into the creative experience.

Guiding and Growing the Whole Child 105

Figure 3.7 Curated, coordinated materials lead to attractive open-ended art
Source: Photo courtesy of Monaire Taylor.

Tips for a Successful Art Program

1 *Teach children how to use materials correctly.* Demonstrate techniques without making a "picture" or product for them to copy. *Children simply cannot do what an adult can do with a pencil or brush; seeing you draw and make things raises the bar too high; they will either pester you to draw things for them or refuse to draw at all. Instead of drawing for them say "Hmm, I wonder what a cat looks like? I know he has a tail"* and then let them work it out.
2 *Teach the routines* that will make the children independent and keep the space reasonably neat. You need to be able to answer these questions:
   - Where are aprons (if necessary) and how do children put them on? Can they hang them up again without help?
   - How/where will names be put onto papers? Is there a pencil handy? Can they write/copy some of the letters in their names? Do they need name cards?
   - Can children reach the things they need and put them away again?
   - Where will they put paper scraps? Will they need a handy sponge?
   - Where do art supplies go when not in use? Are they easy to put away?
   - Is there a nearby place to wash hands?
   - Where will they put finished projects to dry? Can they do this without help?
3 *Use the best quality materials* you can afford and keep them fresh and inviting for the children. For example, paper should be thick enough for the media being

used, muddy paints should be replaced, colored pencils should be sharpened as needed, and glue bottles should not be allowed to clog up.
4   *Teach your class that there are no "right" or "wrong" answers in art.* Avoid judging children's art, even by praising it (even a positive judgment is a judgment because your goal is for the child to value his work regardless of what other people think). Model this for the children by making neutral statements such as:
    - Wow! Look at all those colors!
    - You had to work hard to cut out all these shapes.
    - You made some big long lines and some little marks, too.
    - I wonder how you made that kind of mark?
    - You really enjoyed making that, didn't you?
    - I can see you worked very hard on your picture. Thank you for cleaning up your space for the next artist!
5   *Be realistic.* Some art projects require an extra adult in the room. Some media is better for the end of the year when children are more mature and practiced. Choose materials that fit both the children's and the teacher's ability to handle them with ease.

Open-Ended Art Activities

(Think beforehand about whether you will need a second adult in the room, assigned to this activity, in order for it to be successful.)

Art Center
At a large table (or two tables together) have the following materials available:

- drawing paper
- colored paper (can be different sizes, weights, or textures—use scraps)
- crayons, chalk, oil pastels
- regular and colored pencils
- small glue bottles or glue sticks
- scissors
- wastebasket nearby
- NO coloring books, black-line masters, or dittos! (Put those in your **Writing Center**, along with tracing paper, stencils, and other writing materials.)

RECYCLED ART CENTER

Add the following things to the above to encourage three-dimensional art:

- cardboard TP rolls or larger
- flat pieces of cardboard
- pieces of wrapping paper or fabric

- plastic fruit baskets, bottle caps, small containers and lids
- wood scraps
- other materials that parents bring in—check for sharp edges, etc.
- masking tape or clear tape in an easy-to-use dispenser, glue, scissors.

CRAYON RUBBINGS

Another use for those old broken crayons! First, have children help you peel all the paper off of old crayons. Demonstrate how to place some thin paper (printer paper works) over any textured object, then rub the side of the crayon over it. Add any of the following to the Art Center:

- leaves, especially larger flat ones with textured veins
- cardboard cutouts in different shapes
- screens or mesh
- any flat, textured object.

EASEL PAINTING

Change paint colors with the seasons—begin with primary colors and add more later—mix with white paint to get pastels in spring, etc.:

- easel with easy hooks, clips, or clothespins for children to hang their own papers
- stacked easel paper nearby
- pencil for writing names and name cards if necessary
- paint cups (or milk or yogurt cartons) and one brush for each cup
- tempera paint mixed with liquid starch (cheaper and thicker than plain paint)
- easy-to-use aprons on a nearby hook
- accessible place for paintings to dry (clothesline and pins, countertops, or drying rack).

TABLE PAINTING

All of these tend to be less messy than the easel, but you may still want to use aprons and get a piece of canvas to cover the table top:

- *Q-tip painting*: Put tempera paint in small paper cups (begin with only two colors) and put several Q-tips in each cup. Use only half-sheets of paper. Children sit at table and paint small pictures with Q-tips. Good for holidays, such as using black paper with white and orange paint at Halloween.
- *Sponge painting*: Put tempera paint in flat containers (such as meat trays) and use pieces of old sponges cut in shapes. Attach each sponge to a clothespin for children to hold, and demonstrate using an up–down motion, rather than smearing on the paint.

- *Object printing:* Like sponge painting, except that ordinary objects are used instead of sponges, and clothespins are not required. Objects that make good prints are: cookie cutters, potato mashers, other kitchen implements, any hard (washable) object with an interesting shape.
- *Watercolors:* Instead of watercolor boxes, use colored water (made with food coloring) in little cups and watercolor brushes. Use thicker paper to avoid paint soaking through, or cover table with newspapers.
- *Eye-dropper painting:* Use small cups of colored water as above, but instead of brushes put eye-droppers into the cups. Instead of art paper, use an absorbent paper such as thick paper towels or flat-bottomed coffee filters. Teach children how to use the dropper and drop on a few drops at a time. The color will spread slowly on the paper, and different colors will blend together.
- *Crayon-resist washes*: Children draw pictures with crayons, then go over them with a pale watercolor wash (made with food coloring and water as above). Demonstrate to them that the crayons have to be pressed very firmly to show through the wash. You may want to use crayons that are already broken for this. Children should make their pictures at a different table, then bring them to the wash table to paint.
- *Marble rolling:* Put about an inch of several colors of tempera paint into short paint cups or small bowls. Place a few marbles and a spoon into each cup and put them on a centrally located tray. Put a metal baking pan (like a cake pan) with a paper in it at each seat. The child uses the spoon to scoop a marble out of the cup and drop it onto the paper; by tilting the pan they can roll the marble across the paper, leaving trails and creating a design. When each child is finished, remove the paper to dry and put a new paper in for the next child.

FINGER-PAINTING

Inexpensive finger paint can be made by sprinkling powdered tempura paint over liquid starch. Let the children mix the powder in, or mix two colors. There are two ways to work with this finger paint, both requiring aprons:

- Spoon the finger paint directly onto shiny finger-painting paper.
- Spoon the paint onto cafeteria trays, and when the child is "finished" painting take a print of it by laying regular paper over the paint, pressing, and pulling up.

COLLAGE

Once children have mastered using a glue bottle, there are many variations on this theme:

- *Nature*: Have the children bring in nature artifacts (pine needles, leaves, seeds, small pebbles, etc.). After they have been at the science table for a while, move

them to the art table and show children how to glue them to sturdy paper or cardboard.
- *Colored shapes*: Cut colored paper or fabric scraps into small random shapes and put them in containers by color. Children choose what they want to use to make a design or a picture. (Later in the year, have children cut out their own shapes.)
- *Textures:* Collect items of different textures (may be part of a unit on the five senses) such as fabrics, different kinds of paper, ribbons, sandpaper, yarn, foil, etc. Cut them into small pieces and set out for children to make texture collages.

Sensory Activities

Sensory activities have many of the same benefits as art, but usually with no finished product. They focus on the right side of the brain and often help children to release and control their emotions. If used with props like vehicles or people, they can also stimulate the imagination and language. A variety of containers give children an intuitive understanding of volume, shape, size, weight, and properties of different materials.

Figure 3.8 Sensory play both centers emotions and teaches science
Source: Photo courtesy of Monaire Taylor.

Materials for a Sensory Table or Tub

- plain water
- soap bubble water (swish in dish soap)
- colored water
- sand
- cornmeal, dry beans, rice, lentils
- aquarium gravel
- bird seed
- Oobleck (cornstarch mixed with a small amount of water, food coloring optional)
- Gak/Goo (recipe below).

The Best Playdough Ever

3 cups flour
1½ cups salt
1 Tbsp. cream of tartar
3 cups water
3 Tbsp. vegetable oil
Food coloring.

Mix all ingredients over low heat in a large saucepan, stirring until a ball forms. Let cool, knead until smooth and wrap in plastic. This recipe makes enough for 6–8 children. Roll it into the number of balls desired. It will last for two months if it is kept in an airtight container. It does not need to be refrigerated.

Variations

Make a different color each time.

- For "special" playdough, add colored glitter!
- Change the kinds of toys available for playdough periodically.

Oobleck Recipe

Empty one box of cornstarch into a tub.

Add water, a little at a time, until it reaches a semi-liquid/semi-solid consistency.

Add food coloring if desired.

OR

Mix food coloring into a cup of water and let a child slowly add water until it reaches the consistency he wants.

One of the best features of oobleck is that, while it is satisfyingly messy to play with, *once it dries it can be swept right up.*

Gak Recipe

1. Empty two 4 oz. bottles of white glue (or measure 1 cup) into a bowl.
2. Fill glue bottles with water, shake and empty into the bowl (or measure 1 cup). Add food coloring and mix well. Set aside.
3. Put ½ cup warm water into a plastic cup. Add 1 tsp. Borax and mix until dissolved.
4. Pour water/Borax solution into your glue/water solution and start stirring. Mix with hands until very gelatinous.
5. Store in an airtight container. Enjoy!

Props to add to the sensory table:

- **For pouring and measuring**: containers of different shapes and sizes, plastic tubing, funnels, spoons, colander or sieves, eye-droppers.
- **For washing**: washcloths, small sponges or rags and any rubber dolls, doll clothes, or plastic toys that need washing—best to do outdoors on a sunny day with a clothesline or clean place to put the toys to dry.
- **For imaginative play**: depending on the medium, add small plastic boats or cars and little people, animals, or sea creatures.
- **For fishing**: magnetic fishing poles (short pole with a magnet tied on with string) and a variety of objects, some metal and some not.

Movement and Music

Movement

Teaching children to enjoy music and movement in the classroom is fun and exciting; many children are listening to music, dancing, and singing at home to the delight of their parents. At school the teacher's goal is to set up dancing in a way that helps the children listen to the music and feel the emotion that the music carries as they move. It is important to teach the children to stop dancing when the music stops, and to limit the number of children dancing at one time if the space is limited, to keep this activity within bounds for both children and teacher. Some children can sit and watch while others dance if necessary.

Offer a thoughtful selection of music, some slow and dreamy, some for marching, some classical, some from the musical traditions of different countries. A good concept to teach and have the children able to name is that of "dancer's space," an empty space around each person so each one can move freely. A logical consequence if dancers push or bump into others is that the dancer will need to sit down. Children can dance with scarves and ribbons, they can dance up high or down low, they can dance while lying on their tummies or on their backs. As children get good at dancing and listening they can have many styles going on at the same time—one up high dancer, one down low dancer, and one tummy dancer all dancing together. Dancers can dance fast and dancers can dance slow. Dancers can dance to a song that tells them to hop hop hop, or jump jump jump, and curl up into a ball. Dancers can dance little and get big, or start big and get little. They can do a freeze dance and learn to freeze when the teacher stops the music, then look around and see all the interesting shapes everyone froze in. On a rainy day when bodies have been inside too long you can have a dance party and let everyone dance to rock and roll or popular music. Dancers can have their own orchestra of children who play instruments while they dance; the teacher will need to play a drum to manage the beat and have a signal to stop the musicians from playing. If the teacher is so inclined she can teach the children some exercises and stretches to start or end the dancing.

Unlike a dance class outside of school, the children at school all know each other and the teacher quite well so managing the dancing requires good strategies so the movement does not get out of control or rough. Breaking the class into three groups for a show is one way to keep it under control; one group can be the audience (make tickets, set up chairs), one to be the musicians and decide what songs to sing or play, and what instruments they need to play (air guitar and piano are options), and one to dance. The dancers need to plan the start, middle and end of their dance, what they want to wear, and their bow at the end. If they want to dance a story they will need to tell the musicians so they can match the music to the action. Children love to dance and should have an opportunity right away to learn the rules and to practice as they progress. The three-part show can evolve in fun new directions through the year once they have learned all about how to manage each part. By the end of the year children can be very busy planning and preparing for their dance; it is great fun and may be more about the preparation and planning than the show. In the early years the process is often more interesting than the destination—in dance as in art and most other play.

Music

Music, like art, is an important part of the world of young children. One frequently hears children making up their own songs as they play, humming lullabies to their dolls, or singing favorites at the top of their lungs on the swing. Even if you do not think of yourself as a singer, the children will be happy to hear you sing with them. Children respond to a natural voice: it doesn't have to sound professional, and it can be tuneful even if it's off-key. Our singing voices always sound more attractive than our speaking voices, and children respond to that. If you don't know any good songs for your age group, there are many children's songbooks available, or you can learn some good ones from your colleagues. Acting out simple songs about themselves or their everyday lives ("This in the way we wash our hands ..." or "Mary wore her red shoes ...") are often the favorites of younger preschoolers. Older preschoolers and Kindergarteners enjoy songs about many topics—sailing on the deep blue sea, or dogs with names like B-I-N-G-O—and they love silly songs with hand motions.

Children's love of music can be very helpful in classroom management as well. Do you want them to be quiet and listen? Softly begin chanting their names in a sing-song-y way. This works even better if you sing a phrase such as, "Kirsten is listening to the teacher ... Robert is listening to the teacher ..." Like magic the room becomes quiet as each child waits to hear their own name. On the opposite end of the spectrum, maybe you want the children to burn off extra energy before beginning a lesson. Try playing something lively—either on a CD or with some rhythm instruments—for a few minutes to help them "get the wiggles out." End this activity with a slower piece of music to help them wind down again. Some teachers have "clean-up" songs or soft "resting" songs that cue the children which transition or routine is coming next, or use a call-and-response clapping game (teacher claps a rhythmic pattern and the children clap it back to him) to unify the class and get everybody's attention before starting a whole group activity.

Most children enjoy moving to music in different ways. If you can play a piano or guitar, or even just a drum, you can fit the tempo of the music to the energy in the group. Indoors or outdoors, give them plenty of room to move around and improvise rhythms for jumping, spinning, slow-motion walking, and many other ways to move. There is a real difference in the musical skills at the ages of 4 and 5:

- Four-year-olds will not necessarily follow the tempo of the music. They are more tuned into the energy in their bodies. The way to "improvise" music

with them is to follow their lead and make your rhythm match their energy level.
- Five-year-olds have more motor control than 4s, as well as a greater desire to conform to adult standards. With this age group, they can more easily manage to follow the rhythm set by the teacher.

Opportunities to quietly listen to different kinds of music, and let the music speak directly to the child's imagination, are valuable experiences in every classroom. The skill of listening to music is one that can be taught. Begin the lesson at a quiet time, such as a resting time after lunch or vigorous outdoor play. Have the children sitting on the rug or comfortably resting at their seats or on mats. Have handy some different kinds of short recorded music without words. If you can find a recording with short snippets of classical music, you can play one or two of them every day. Or, try some flute or guitar solos that aren't too long, and branch out from there. Model the behavior you want to see: show the children that you are listening attentively to the music and enjoying it. Just let the music speak directly to the children without any clapping in time or discussion about what you hear. Each child will experience it differently. They may not be able to put into words what they are feeling, so it is important that the teacher does not impose her own interpretation on what they hear. You are giving them a gift, and what they do with it is up to them.

Modified Play to Support Academics

A few months into the year, or perhaps sooner in Kindergarten, teachers will have assessed their students' academic skills and found them to cover a broad continuum. Just like the social skills that were discussed in the section on helping children to make friends, academic skills are also a combination of maturity (brain development) and past experience (opportunities to practice). Children with little experience with books, or pre-literacy or pre-numeracy activities, will obviously be in a different place than children who are a little older and have had more exposure to letters and numbers. Some children will zoom along in acquiring letter names, but need more time to get good at counting, and vice-versa. In Chapter 6 you will see how these varying needs may be addressed by forming small, intense—and above all, flexible—intervention groups to receive direct instruction tailored to their needs.

Here we address another important question: what are the other children doing while the teacher is working with a small group? Sometimes the teacher is lucky enough to have an assistant or volunteer parent who can assist in supervision. Many times, the teacher is the only adult in her classroom. In the past, teachers have solved this problem by giving the other students coloring pages, copying exercises, or easy worksheets to keep them quiet and busy while the teacher is working with the small group (which is where the teacher is giving the most value to the children who need her support). Or they have set up table activities and used a timer to rotate the groups every 10 or 15 minutes. In either case, the children are taught to handle this time of the day with minimal adult direction.

Recent research tells us that there is another way this can be accomplished which is more in line with how young children learn. We know that children are active learners and that the most efficient way for them to integrate all the parts of their brains is through play. The National Association for the Education of Young Children (NAEYC) recommends that a "significant part of their day" should be play-based. In fact, a recent experiment in the Fort Worth, Texas school system showed that more time for recess and movement during the day improved the ability of students to focus and pay attention in class when it is time to listen.

The most elegant solution is one that meets children's individual needs, honors their need to move around and choose what they will be working on (play is the work of children)—while at the same time is easy to manage even if there is only one adult in the room. This approach is to offer children two different kinds of play at different times of the day:

- The first is a regular playtime, which usually works best in the morning when children are fresh, includes blocks, dramatic play, and art activities, as well as other interest centers. During this playtime the teacher is observing the play, assessing children's development, and teaching social/emotional skills as the need arises.
- The second play period, perhaps in the afternoon, offers quieter activities and—as the year goes on—perhaps more academically oriented activities as well. The teacher only works with intervention groups during this second playtime. In Kindergarten, children who are already beginning to read might have a reading group with the teacher at this time.

Most of Chapter 3 has been about the first play period and how to help children get the most out of their morning play period. This section is about centers and routines that will make the second play period most productive. Having two different kinds of play periods works best in an all-day program. Remember that the main purpose of this second playtime is to help children who need more academic instruction to move up to grade level as quickly as possible ... children who need more social and emotional development will benefit more from the guided playtime than from small intervention groups. The smaller the intervention group, and the more focused the teacher is on covering only one skill at a time, the more powerful the intervention will be.

Before beginning an intervention program, consider the maturity level of your children. Half a year's difference in age and development really matters! Younger 4s still have a greater need for active play, and want to see what their friends are doing. Four-year-old brains are not yet compartmentalized enough to focus on academic skills in a vacuum. They learn best by experimenting with real things—that is, while playing. That is why the section on infusing their play activities with literacy and numeracy is recommended, especially for PreK children. Their school readiness needs can also be met in short whole-group activities, such as listening and chiming in as the teacher reads ABC books, learning songs, poems, and chants, or counting how many children, how many chairs, how many stripes on the flag, as a whole group, led by the teacher. The key to success with 4-year-olds is to keep whole-group instruction short and interactive.

In a class of older 4-year-olds, such as a transitional Kindergarten, children may not be ready for intervention groups until January (as the children are turning 5). Kindergarteners can begin learning the following routines earlier in the year, depending on the composition of the class. In a combination PreK/K class, the Kindergarteners will be ready to work independently at some simple independent "Kindergarten" centers while the PreK students are playing at quiet activities in the afternoon. The teacher can pull a few Kindergarteners at a time for intervention during this time. Or, an instructional assistant can supervise the PreK students as they play while the teacher covers the Kindergarten curriculum.

Tips for preparing children for the "modified playtime":

1   For the children who are playing, choose activities that the children are familiar with and can handle without adult help. Some good choices are simple art activities such as drawing with crayons or colored pencils; creative cut and paste (not following a pattern); easier puzzles and table toys such as Legos, small blocks, or other math manipulatives; simple lotto games or matching games; BINGO with letters or numbers; retelling favorite books to dolls or teddy bears; recreating felt board stories with a friend; tracing paper and pictures or letters to trace over; playdough and cookie cutters; a miniature dollhouse to play with a friend; stringing beads or buttons, and other fine motor activities.

2   The independent centers/play activities work best if the students are allowed to choose what they want to do and can put away their materials independently before going to a new activity. It is best to let the children stay with an activity as long as they are engaged with it; rotating groups arbitrarily interrupts their explorations and does not allow free choice. There should be enough activities available to provide variety and choice, but not so many that cleanup will be a problem. Every week or two, change some of the activities. Later in the year, Kindergarteners may enjoy choosing to do simple worksheets or practice reading books they are familiar with. The operative word is "choose." Children will try harder and stay longer at activities they have chosen for themselves.

3   Begin by teaching a special routine for this time of day. When activities are well aligned to the children's interests and abilities, and the children know the

routines of putting away activities when they are done, the only *new* routine will be "not interrupting the teacher," allowing you to work closely with an intervention group. Some teachers use a visible reminder, such as a STOP sign or a special hat, that tells the children not to interrupt for anything but an emergency. This routine of "solving your own problems" needs to be thoroughly taught and practiced before the teacher can begin to work with a small group. (If you consistently have another adult in the room to help the "players" you will not need this routine.)

4   Introduce the "solving your own problems" routine as something they are now old enough (or smart enough, or grown-up enough) to do on their own. Most children—especially 5-year-olds—like to feel grown-up. Introduce the centers and tell them that they will have to manage without asking the teacher to help them. If something is too hard, or there is a problem they can't solve, it will be okay to put that toy or game away and try something else. Or they can ask a friend to help them, or … have them brainstorm how they can solve a problem on their own. Tell them that you will be watching their play, but will not help them. You will be taking notes to see how well they do. The first play period may only be five or ten minutes—you want them to be successful!

5   After the practice period, call the children together to "debrief" their experience. Begin by asking what went well: Who played nicely? Who remembered to put their toys away? Were there any problems? How could they be solved? Of course, you would have been watching, so you know who did well and what the problems were. This can be a good way to fine-tune the routine as you go. In one classroom, the "problem" was that a pencil point broke and the children were not allowed to use the pencil sharpener. What to do? The teacher solved it by providing a container of sharpened pencils in an accessible place so that children could get another one if needed.

6   Repeat this practice time for about a week, gradually increasing the time, and continuing to observe it. When you feel that most children are doing well, you can try calling a small group to your table for about five minutes, and see how that works. Adjust as needed. Your goal is to get about a half-hour of quiet time—enough for you to call three small groups. Keep reinforcing the behavior you want to see, rather than talking about problems. That will establish "good behavior" as the way to get attention in your classroom.

Troubleshooting

If there are continuing problems, analyze to find the cause.

- Is it just one or two children who can't seem to work independently? Sometimes a child just needs to be close to the teacher. Bring a special activity for that child to your intervention table and have that child work on it at your table or on the rug nearby as you work with a small group.

- Is it a particular activity that is either too difficult or too popular? Change it for something else that is less problematic ... or think of whether a popular activity can successfully be made available for more children by adding more materials, expanding the space, etc.
- Is the whole class having difficulty? Maybe there were too many or too few choices. Maybe the time was too long. Maybe the activities were not engaging enough. If you can't solve it, back up, wait a few weeks, and then try again. Some classes just have more children who need time to learn how to get along with each other. A class like this will benefit from more practice with teacher-guided play as they learn how to get along; remember, that is a part of the foundation for all academic learning.

Maintenance

You have finally trained your class and you are enjoying seeing the progress being made by the children you have been working with. Then ... things begin to deteriorate. The play is getting louder, there are more interruptions, and somehow this is just not working anymore. Here are some tips to keep this from happening.

- Once the children have been trained in the routine and are doing well, do not abandon the "debriefing" after each session. It can be very short if things are going well. The children like to tell the teacher what they were doing, so call on two or three children to tell the class what they did. Done. You can also use this time to praise any cooperative behavior that you noticed.
- If things are not going too well, don't let it deteriorate further: have a longer debrief and nip that problem in the bud. First, revisit the troubleshooting. How long has it been since you changed the activities? Who or what is causing this problem? Address it right away.
- If the problem continues, or has already gotten out of control, go all the way back to step one of training. Stop pulling groups for one week and retrain the children in the "solving my own problems" routine. The benefits the children get from learning how to handle themselves independently are well worth the effort!

Reflection on Chapter 3

1. As a multi-tasking teacher of young children, which of the following "hats" fit you comfortably? (Check as many as apply.)
   - ☐ observing the children and the play.
   - ☐ guiding the play to help children develop social skills and self-control.
   - ☐ noticing and assessing children's skills while observing them play.
   - ☐ infusing your interest centers with opportunities to practice using letters and numbers.
   - ☐ creating and managing smooth transitions.
   - ☐ enabling children to manage their own environment (teaching routines).
   - ☐ fostering two-way communication with parents and other adults.
   - ☐ other _____
   _____

2. Not all hats will fit you the same. Look at this list again, and choose one or two skills that you would like to work on in the coming year. Choose the one(s) that you feel will have the most positive results in your classroom. Write them here:

   I would like to become better at _____
   _____

   because _____
   _____

   My secondary goal is to improve _____
   _____

   because _____
   _____

3. If you have not taught this age group before, or have done it very differently, it will take more than one school year to master this way of teaching. Be kind to yourself! Take baby steps and celebrate your accomplishments. Each new school year is a gift: a time to start over with different children and a clean slate. Write here your ideas for how you would like to keep track of your own growth as a teacher of young children, and how you plan to celebrate your accomplishments.

Chapter 4

The Art of Teaching Self-Control

Key Information in this Chapter
- Using discipline to teach self-control
- Appropriate discipline for young children
- Preventing and addressing challenging behavior

Prevention, not Punishment

Teaching is such a big, multi-faceted job! The teacher's influence touches every child in her classroom, especially in these early years. Before we knew what we now do about the developing child, the growth of the brain, and the increase in understanding this growth brings to the child, people commonly used scolding, shaming and physical punishment to change children's immature behavior. Today, educators know that these old-fashioned methods only temporarily control children and fail to help children learn to manage and control themselves. When children's behavior is externally controlled by adults, the unwanted behavior returns as soon as the adult is gone. Unless children learn how to control their own behavior, they will continue to make mistakes on a bigger and more dangerous scale as the years go by.

The old punitive systems addressed behavior *after* it happened, but even Benjamin Franklin knew that "An ounce of prevention is better than a pound of cure." In the early years when we are teaching children to learn to manage and be responsible for their own behavior, addressing the root of disruptive behavior and preventing it is more successful than humiliating children who make mistakes. Today, society asks teachers to include younger children in the school-age experience, for longer hours than ever before. Teachers, in partnership with parents, are indeed part of the village that it takes to raise a child, sharing responsibility for guiding the young brain to both appropriately meet the needs of the children and accommodate societal needs.

Teaching a 5-year-old to be responsible for her actions and to listen to adults is much easier than teaching a 13-year-old to be responsible for her actions and listen to the adults, and much, much easier and less expensive than trying to teach an

18-year-old the same lesson. The positive discipline techniques that follow offer guidance in how to align with the needs of the young child's development while teaching her self-control. After children have developed more mature brains, have more practice and ability to control their impulses, and have developed some conscience, these internal controls will always be with them. Young children simply need time, guidance, and experience to learn to do better. A strong relationship with a teacher who knows how to teach the children social and emotional skills through their play is the ounce of prevention needed to prevent pounds of cure. This is why economists say that every dollar invested in high quality early childhood education saves at least seven dollars in later costs of remediation.

Teaching Social and Emotional Competence

Interpersonal conflict is frequently the result of misunderstood intentions and messages that end up in hurt feelings and/or aggressive behavior. Sensitive observation by the teacher is the first strategy in teaching social and emotional competence, which requires the ability to care for one's own needs and those of others, while relating to other people in an open, kind, thoughtful and friendly way. This is our goal for all children as well as for ourselves.

We want children to know that people generally mean well, but sometimes do make mistakes. This message relieves the child of any worry that there is something personal about the problems that arise in play. We are creating a baseline in the child's social responses so we want to help the children see that it is normal for us to have social mix-ups, and normal for us to be able to clarify them. We want the child calm enough to access his higher brain, think the situation through, and control his responses. We want the child free of fear, which may ensure compliance but rarely leads to constructive learning. The teacher makes the classroom safe, does not allow the children to coerce or raise their voices at each other, and treats children respectfully even when she is frustrated or unhappy with their behavior. Because the teacher avoids scolding, yelling or shaming, the children learn constructive, positive language that will facilitate communication—even when they are upset. When the teacher says "Oh no! Let's clean it up," to the child who knocked over the vase of flowers on her desk, she models how to respond when your artwork is ruined by a cup of spilled paint. Teaching the children to say "I'm busy now, I'll play with you later" instead of "Go Away!" gives the children positive, constructive language that communicates their intentions ("It's not that I don't like you or never want to play with you, but really I'm in the middle of something now that I just want to do with this person"). The child who hears "Go Away!" is likely to come back with a negative emotional response that moves the whole discussion way off track—suddenly the child who was happily playing has been pulled off course to defend himself from a child who took his words personally and got mad.

Young children have difficulty seeing another child's point of view. Other children's behavior feels unpredictable to them even when we, as adults, can anticipate that Action X will likely lead to Outcome Y. Even if we disagree with a child's behavior, we can help other children to see that what they do is predictable and logical. The teacher can say: "He feels just like you do when other people are not listening. Soon he'll get mad, and then you know there could be some yelling and even hitting. It would be best to stop doing that and start listening, so you can talk and figure out what to do now." Knowing that behavior makes sense eliminates the natural fear children feel when they can't anticipate, let alone control, what might happen next.

Constant opportunities to teach social and emotional skills come up when a group of children plays together; in fact, it is one of the main reasons that a play experience is so important for young children. Social and emotional competence can only be learned in relationship to other people, with coaching from more mature members of the culture, and is the foundation for self-control—which, as we saw in Chapter 1, is the foundation for all learning.

Figure 4.1 This companionship reflects a trusting relationship
Source: Photo courtesy of Geraldine Rocha.

Discipline

Discipline means teaching children new ideas about how to solve problems, with the focus on helping them learn to manage themselves. The teacher wants to provide tools that allow the child to drop the behavior that is not working in favor of more socially acceptable behavior. As we saw in Chapter 1, this is a key skill for success. Teachers and parents will not always be with children when trouble arises, so our goal must be to teach children to manage when caring adults are not there to help them. We want to teach children to act in thoughtful, responsible ways because they find it positive and successful, not out of guilt, fear, or shame. If the child obeys the teacher only out of fear of punishment, she will only behave well when the teacher is present.

Teachers set limits and teach children self-discipline in many ways. In a large classroom with many children, discipline often starts in the form of external control on the part of the teacher who must create order and keep the children safe even before they know her. Most children have an attached relationship with a primary adult or two in their lives and when they get to know the teacher they naturally transfer this understanding of relationship to their teacher. When this occurs the teacher can begin teaching children to control their own behavior, even when he or she is not around, because the children learn that controlling themselves brings them the results they want. Helping the children develop self-discipline is the goal in PreK and Kindergarten classrooms.

"Natural consequences" is a strong incentive for self-discipline, as the child learns that her behavior leads to a result, and that the result relates to a choice the child is making. For example, a child who persists in hitting other children may not be invited to play with them; the teacher can help the child understand that since the others don't like being hit she will have to play alone until she can remember not to hit. The teacher is helping the child learn the connection between her behavior, her relationship to others, and her ability to enjoy the privileges of choosing for herself.

The best discipline or limit is the kind that the child can hold onto when the teacher isn't there. These are some guiding principles for the teacher:

- Children are not here to please teachers. They are here to learn how to manage on their own when the teacher is not with them.
- Consistency is very important.
- Stay objective and, when it is safe, allow natural consequences. Be sure the child knows why the situation is not working and help him find a solution.
- Try not to react emotionally or to take things personally.
- Give children the information that hurting others does not work as a form of communication. Other children don't know what they want when they hit or hurt. Other children will get mad, cry, yell, or even hit back when they get hit. What works better is using a friendly voice to say what they want so the other person can hear what is being said.

A common strategy of young, socially inept children is to try to control another child's behavior. They want to be friends, but another child's behavior is much less predictable than that of an adult. Four-year-olds do this in more overt ways—"You have to be the baby because I'm the mom!"—followed by the teacher reminding the "controller" that everyone gets to choose for themselves. Fives may learn to be more subtle. When children chase each other and catch and hug or kiss the caught child, this teasing behavior can be a hidden attempt to dominate and control the other child. When this behavior pops up it is useful to call a meeting between the children so you can help the children communicate, listen, and get to know one another; it is immature and insecure behavior, and a wonderful teaching opportunity. Think about how you want to guide the meeting while letting the children express themselves and have a meaningful conversation. Asking open-ended questions will help you gain information: "It doesn't look like he likes it when you kiss him; I wonder why you are doing that when he doesn't want you to?"

Teachers may need to untangle misunderstandings, especially when the children are learning how to play with others and emotion overrides their ability to use their upper brain reasoning. Help the child know what to say, and affirm how the child was feeling. A teacher sees trouble brewing in the block area and comes closer to see what is causing the trouble. "Were you worried that Alex was going to take your toy when his hand came so close to where you were playing?" To the other child she would ask: "Were you going to put your hand on Karen's toy? Oh, you were just getting that truck near her." Back to the first child: "Alex wasn't going to touch your things. He was getting the truck." Back to Alex, say: "You can tell him you want the truck."

If this situation had already escalated into hitting, you will put natural consequences into play. Children who hit others need to play alone for a while because no one wants to play with someone who hits him. In that case, you will tell Karen, "You were worried and your hand went out and hit, and hitting doesn't work. Too bad, but now you are done playing here because it's not okay to hurt other people. You will need to find someplace else to play; you'll remember next time." If you feel that Alex actually was provoking Karen, they are both redirected to another area or toy.

To help children who don't seem to be listening when you are talking to them, or when so much emotion is present that the child can't listen well, have the child tell you back what you just said to her. This will help you know that the child heard you and can help her stop herself by internalizing the language. If the situation occurs again you can remind her that this is a repeat offense and strengthen the consequence: "It seems like I need to choose for you right now. You can go look at a book now; I'll come by the book area and tell you when you can try choosing for yourself again." (Of course you want children to have pleasant feelings about books; you know that Karen loves books and will find it centering to look at them quietly. A child who has not yet formed that relationship with books might be given playdough to play with in a quiet corner. Your goal is not to make the child miserable, but for the child to feel the consequence of not being allowed to make her own choice because she chose badly by hitting.)

You can also tell a child that when he feels ready, he can ask the teacher if it is okay for him to come back and try again. This is not an apology, it is an agreement: "I think I can do better if you let me try again." The teacher can say, "I don't think that is a good idea right now; there are too many children playing there. I don't think I will be able to help you remember to move the blocks carefully. You can try again another time when there are not so many children playing here," or you can say "Yes, I can stay close so I can help you if you need me. Tell me again, what it is you are going to remember?" The child answers: "I won't knock the blocks over." "Oh that's right, I think you can remember that this time."

If you take something away be sure to suggest another activity. Bored children tend to get into trouble.

Positive Redirection and Setting Limits

Positive redirection should be used whenever possible. It is based on the premise that children want to be good, but don't always know how. While it seems obvious to an adult that "stop shouting" means "lower your voice," children who are upset cannot instantly make that connection so the teacher says "When you speak quietly the other children can understand you better." So instead of saying "no" and "don't," tell the child what you do want him to do. The child who is taking others' things can be reminded "You can choose any toy on the shelf." (For more about helpful, positive language see Chapter 5.)

However, when a child's behavior is dangerous to himself or others, he needs to be stopped. The teacher must let the child know gently, but firmly, that he will not be allowed to hurt himself or others. Children who rarely hear words like "Stop!" or "No!" will quickly respond when they do hear them—another reason the teacher holds these words in reserve for urgent situations. When an adult sets this kind of limit on behavior, the child's fears of his own impulses will be assuaged and the child will build more trust in the teacher's ability to help him.

When setting a limit on a child's behavior, remember that young children are still learning how to behave, and their concepts of time and consequences are not yet fully developed. The following are *age-appropriate* ways to set a limit:

- Both the limit and the reason for it must be clear to the child: "I can't let you throw the blocks because if they hit someone it will really hurt. You'll need to come play someplace else now to help you remember, so that won't happen again. Next time you want to throw you can look for the beanbags."
- The consequence for breaking a limit needs to be in the moment—immediate consequences or redirection—no threats of consequences that will happen

"later." This is because children live in the moment; later consequences are only weakly connected to the unwanted behavior. The delay can make the teacher's actions seem arbitrary.
- Feelings are more important than facts—rather than focusing on blame, say, "you forgot" or "you made a mistake" and "how can we fix it?" End the conversation by saying, "Next time you'll remember to ..." and state the preferred, positive behavior.
- Hurting is never justified. A child who hurts another (even for a "good reason") cannot play in that area any more today. It is entirely appropriate for a child to feel sad about that; feeling sad is the experience that will help him remember not to do it again. Still, the teacher can demonstrate empathy by saying "Too bad, I'm sorry that happened. But you can try again tomorrow and then you'll remember." The child receives the message that even though privileges were curtailed the teacher is on his side, and he also hears her expression of faith in his ability to do better in the future.
- Avoid taking away playtime or recess; remember that these are the important times for children to build the very skills you want them to work on. What you can do is take away the privilege of choosing what you want to do during playtime for the rest of that period, by assigning the child to stay at an activity you select. Sensory activities, such as water play, cornmeal, or playdough are good choices, as they help the child to calm down. Art can also be a good choice, if the child enjoys it, because art provides a way of expressing strong feelings.

Follow through! It may be inconvenient to stay and see that the child is honoring the limit that was set, but it is necessary. A teacher's actions speak louder than words; avoid suggesting consequences you might not be able to follow through on or you lose credibility for the next encounter.

Progressive Discipline for Kindergarten

Progressive discipline is a plan that the teacher makes ahead of time in case she finds herself alone in a difficult situation during direct instruction. Dealing with a defiant or upset child can be stressful, but most of the stress (for the teacher) comes from not knowing what to do next. A teacher who already has a plan knows what she will do step by step; this helps the teacher to stay calm even if the child is very emotional. Here is a sample progressive discipline plan that would be appropriate for 5-year-olds while the teacher is giving whole group instruction to the class. Although it is unlikely that it would be needed in a preschool setting, it can be adapted to different school systems.

This scenario is an example of external control used by the teacher for the good of the whole class because the child is so disruptive that positive learning cannot occur. In a group of

4-year-olds, a similar problem could be handled by having another adult quietly take the child to another area of the room, or by cutting the lesson short, then returning to it at a later time.

1. The teacher gives the child one clear reminder, explanation, or redirection to change her behavior.
2. The teacher observes to see that the child's behavior is changing. Following through is essential. A teacher who has good rapport with the children will probably smile at the child if the disruptive behavior has stopped.
3. If the disruptive behavior continues, seating a child closer to the teacher during a lesson may help the behavior to improve. Or, the teacher might say, "You are having a hard time today. Do you need some time out to think about things?" Offer the Quiet Corner, but don't insist.

> The Quiet Corner is a place for one child who needs time to get control of his feelings. It might have a pillow or rocking chair, a stuffed animal, a picture book about feelings, or other aids to help the child calm down. It is not a "time out" imposed by the teacher, but a place the child chooses when he is feeling overwhelmed. The child can stay as long as he needs to, then re-enter the group when he is ready.

4. In either case, if the behavior continues to escalate (as it may in a child who is intent on testing the teacher's limits, or with a child who is beginning to lose control) the child is put on notice: "You need to be quiet so other children can listen." This is followed by "If you can't be quiet so the others can listen, you will have to leave the classroom." At this point the teacher may seat the child in a chair behind the group, where the child can still see the lesson, but other children will not be able to see what the child is doing. (Sometimes the lack of an audience defuses attention-getting behavior.)
5. If the problem continues, the teacher sends the child to a buddy classroom (arranged ahead of time with another teacher) or to the office, according to school protocol, and lets the parent know there was a problem.
6. After the child returns from time out of the classroom, the teacher needs to repair the relationship. Having a quiet talk about what happened and why should end on a positive note. She might say, "I know you don't like to be in trouble, and I don't like it either. Next time, let's try to solve the problem so that you can stay in the classroom. I like to have you here!"
7. Follow up by talking to the parent: Is the child getting enough sleep? Is there a problem at home? Try to problem-solve as a team with the parent to find the cause of the child's behavior.

Challenging Behavior

Schools have a multitude of systems and policies for working with children who exhibit challenging behaviors. In many situations overarching school policies take neither the young child's immature brain, nor his limited ability to actually manage his own behavior without adult support, into account. This can be especially challenging when a class for 4-year-olds is added on to an elementary school; what seem like reasonable expectations for the behavior of children in school become unreasonable when they are the same for 4-year-olds and 10-year-olds. All children make mistakes and get confused about rules and responsibilities; all children can become emotional and forget to behave in civilized ways. As much as adults may prefer not to see this behavior, it is in fact normal and offers a teaching opportunity which will serve the child more constructively than punishment.

The brain comes pre-programmed for survival, and young children know they are vulnerable and cannot survive without adult support. Children under 6 are thus simultaneously egocentric (only seeing things from their own point of view) and intensely focused on reading adult reactions. Morality, ethics, and the development of a conscience await further development of the brain in the areas of logic, ability to understand abstract consequences, and the capacity for reflection and reason. The ability to manage and control feelings and impulses is fleeting. When working with children between the ages of 4 and 6 it is the adult that guides and co-controls the child's behavior—with the child's permission, trust and cooperation. This is why it is so important to build a relationship early in the year with every child; young children are not likely to care what you think of them unless they know and care about their relationship with you.

Building self-awareness and learning to manage feelings is the foundation on which children develop empathy as well as the social and emotional skills that will bring success in school and life—a key part of the curriculum of the PreK and Kindergarten child. Feelings are often overwhelming, confusing, and messy. They will not go away if left unaddressed, but instead will seep out in mean, cutting behavior, sarcasm, aggression, inappropriate competition, obesity, substance abuse and depression. Challenging behavior often provides the teachable moment to help children learn to identify their feelings and develop strategies to manage the behavior triggered by those feelings.

Temperament always needs to be part of the analysis of a child's behavior, as inborn temperament affects children's responses to different situations. In a group of newborn babies it is quickly apparent that each comes with its own way of responding to the world. Some seem to relish movement and action, while others are quickly distressed when the room around them gets too busy. Such inborn traits filter every experience the child will have in life, and in the early years every child is learning how they affect his interactions with other people and experiences. Teachers and parents help him learn how to be true to himself while also moderating his behavior to conform with cultural expectations. The child who is anxious in a busy room learns strategies to cope with a room full of peers rather than yell at them to be quiet. The child who loves action learns to be still and focus now and then. Recognizing and valuing these innate traits builds the child's self-esteem when the teacher can help him learn to harness and channel them—"You can really move, will you run across the yard for that ball?" Each temperament trait carries both a negative and positive connotation, a persistent child can be seen as stubborn but also as determined (more likely to solve a hard problem), a cautious child can seem overly timid but also can be trusted not to climb too high up a tree.

Impulsive behavior "just happens" from the child's perspective; it is a "primitive brain stem" response that does not involve analysis or thought, and comes up more often with 4-year-olds than 5s. "Feral" behavior is the result of an overwhelming impulse; biting, hitting and scratching are rarely planned but come from a desperate feeling that triggers impulsive action. Even if a child says, "I'm going to bite you" she usually means that she is worried that she might bite, not that she plans to. The brain has evolved to shut down access to higher functions in a moment of crisis, leaving the lower brain in charge. When adults say "But she knows better; she just told me this morning that she would tell me what's wrong instead of biting," they are describing the difference between information from the neo-cortex and action initiated by the brain stem. In a calm discussion she is able to engage her higher-level thinking, which reminds her not to bite, but in the emotion-clouded moment her behavior is dictated by the brain stem. (The adult can gain compassion for the child in this situation by recalling a time when, as a fully mature adult, you have been so upset that you could not speak but could only cry or yell or clench your fists. Most of us can also recall a time in childhood when someone demanded "What were you thinking?" after we behaved badly—and we honestly could not answer because we were not thinking, just primitively responding.)

Causes and Consequences

To help a child, the teacher must question and analyze the situation. Why is this child feeling so stressed and out of control? In many cases, the teacher can get this information from *observation*: what happens right before this behavior occurs? When the teacher recognizes the conditions that typically lead to injury she can step right in and slow down the situation, giving the child a chance to control her behavior. In some cases, the teacher may need more information from parents: Have there been any new stresses at home? A new baby, talk about moving, a pending divorce, a death, or other family events can lead to acting-out behavior in school. Notice if the child is getting overwhelmed; when information, expectations and a shortage of self-regulation all converge at once, whether in play or in a lesson, it can overwhelm the brain's immature ability to manage. It can be helpful to chart when behavior occurs or note if the child is tired, over-extended, out-maneuvered by older children, hungry, etc. Some of these conditions are easy to fix or avoid and will eliminate the problem.

The teacher needs to stay calm, objective, and in her center in the presence of the child's big emotion. This shows the child that he is safe with the teacher, and keeps the emotion with the child and his behavior. By staying calm she is also more able to keep her wits about her and guide the child from her thoughtful, caring, objective mind.

Strategy One—Holding the Teacher's Hand

When children appear to be out of control, one thing the teacher can do is simply tell the child "It looks like you need my help; come hold my hand and I'll help you." Simply hold the child's hand as you go about your business. This is a consequence that takes away the child's freedom to self-initiate. It is not harsh or humiliating, but it is firm and clear; you are not managing your behavior (i.e., listening to others, keeping your body safe, remembering to use words, respecting other children's space, etc.), and when I see that it makes me think you need my help. I'll hold your hand so we can stay close and I can help you. The help you are giving is that of helping the child to regulate—a term from the mental health world that describes the ability to stay balanced and exercise self-control. Your calm adult presence offers external regulation (think of a parent rocking a baby and singing a lullaby—the parent is externally regulating) to the child and brings her back to her center. As the teacher you can't stop doing what you need to do, so hold the child's hand and have the child follow along while you teach. The child will see lots of children engaged and busy, and the teacher keeping her focus on the positive behavior of the other children. Pretty soon the child will realize she would rather get busy herself, and would really rather not hold the teacher's hand. When the child decides she would rather be doing something else, ask her to tell you what she is planning to do, and what she needs to remember so she won't need to come back and hold your hand again? Praise her for remembering and say "That's right, you'll remember next time!" The teacher's goal is for the child to realize what she did that did not work for her, and remember what she needs to do—saying this out loud is helpful and will help the child work to control herself to avoid future consequences.

Strategy Two—An Immediate Redirect

A child who bites needs a bite-able object readily available, like a teething bracelet on her wrist. Providing a safe place to hit or bite serves as an intermediate step when a child has a physical urge that she cannot yet stop. Pillows should be nearby for a child who hits, or a chewable toy for one who bites. The teacher can say, "Here is something you can hit so nobody gets hurt." Parents can be asked to keep fingernails trimmed short on a child who scratches. These are interim measures, because ultimately you do want the child to be able to manage herself, but in the short term it is a success when nobody gets hurt. Remember, the child whose physical reactions are too powerful for her to stop needs your help and really can't change the behavior without adult guidance plus her own maturation and learning. She will learn more quickly and happily if she is not in trouble all the time!

Strategy Three—Choosing for the Child

Set up an area where you can isolate the child who has hurt someone. This offense is more drastic so requires a stronger limit; the consequence of hurting others is that the teacher chooses where you will play, what you can do, and when you are able to rejoin the class. The child is removed from the group to allow her to regroup and to keep others safe. Ideally, this space provides the child with a centering activity like playdough to pound, a book to look at, or crayons to scribble, that will calm the child.

Revisit the Problem Later

Children still live so "in the moment" that they can feel that they will stay mad or scared forever, not realizing that feelings come and go and they do not have to control them. No one likes to be out of control and make a scene; children feel embarrassed and ashamed and helpless when this happens to them. The last step is to talk about what happened, when the child is calm and able to think and express himself, and make a plan so it will not happen again. This should be a clear, objective conversation, without judgment or scolding, about exactly what happened and why that behavior doesn't work and never will. The goal is to help the child understand and try to think before he acts next time; putting the problem and solutions into words moves the situation out of the lower brain and into the higher brain where the child can access it.

Helping the child learn to notice where he feels emotion rise in his body will begin to help him get in front of the flood of feeling and related behavior. The teacher can ask "Where is it inside? How does it feel just before the mad comes? Does your jaw get tight? Does your face feel hot? Does your tummy feel sick?" The teacher's clarity about what happened to cause the trouble, why the behavior won't work, the consistent consequence devoid of teacher judgment, the final message about what behavior the teacher does want, and her expectation that the child can do this, helps the child actually take responsibility for his actions and turn them around. The teacher can sympathize: "That's too bad that happened, let's work on not letting it happen again."

To help this child build his social and emotional skills the teacher must build her relationship with him; he has to feel that his teacher is on his side 100 percent, ready to help him get past this problem. The teacher can say something like "Remember how upset you got when your friend got scratched and didn't want to play anymore? That was too bad and you felt sad; I even heard some crying. You'll remember next time about the scratching problem and use your words. If you feel that mad coming you'll go quick and get a drink of water and I'll be close if you need me. We'll work it out so that scratching won't happen and you can stay and hear our story, and the children will like sitting near you." With consistent support, the child will begin to internalize this new system and see that he has a choice and control over his behavior, and someone is there to help him with it.

Soon the child will be able to stop himself long enough to come straight to the teacher so she can help, or go to the book area and hit a stuffed animal, or go to the stress balls and choose one to squeeze, or get a drink of water. The children know what will help them so let them tell you what they think will be best. They will inevitably get mad and forget their plan some of the time before they master this, and then you can honestly say "Oh darn, that is so disappointing; I really wish you had remembered to keep your hands back. Oh well, come play a little by yourself over here; I'll find a toy for you and later we can talk about it." Let the child calm down in the "teacher chooses" area and then remind him that next time he will do better and will remember his plan.

Under normal circumstances and with typically developing children this system works very well. It is slow and humane with its constructive focus. At first children may not seem to mind losing their privileges, because after all there are lots of other things to do, but the more their behavior interferes with their free choice the more they will try to control their behavior. You will see other children helping too, "Do you want to play in the blocks with me? Remember not to kick the blocks so we can keep playing, okay?" Teachers can remind them too: "If you want to play here with Tasha, what do you need to remember so we won't have trouble like last time? That's right, keep your hands back and tell her what you want so there won't be any pushing. Tasha, can Susie play with you if she remembers to keep her hands back and use her words?"

The Goal is Always Self-Control

The teacher's goal is to teach the children to control themselves so they can successfully manage when she is not around to help. Teachers and parents may see the same behavior over and over again because the reaction it gets works for the child on some level. The child's definition of what works may be quite different from the teacher's—sometimes, simply getting someone's undivided attention counts as a success even when it is angry attention. *Things that work for the child quickly become a habit, so it is the teacher's job to stop the habit from working.* Hitting, biting, pulling hair, pinching, scratching, or generally hurting others are really all powerful ways to quickly get what you want. The effective response is to insist that the child communicate using words rather than pain, and to set clear consequences. If hurting others really works for the child it can easily become a habit to allow the

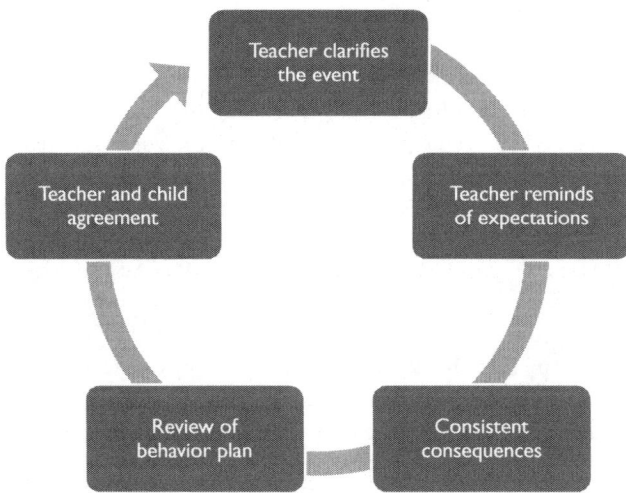

Figure 4.2 Helping children develop self-control

impulse to rule the child's behavior; clear, consistent limits will stop it from working. Luckily a clear consequence and a class agreement to use your words and tell children to say what they want can have a big impact.

The teacher can help him understand that he can learn to manage his behavior, and she can help by reminding him of that when she sees the dysregulation coming. Next time a child cuts in front of him in the line for the slide he will feel his hand form a fist and remember to punch the sand instead of the child. Ideally, the teacher is right there to congratulate him for his progress.

As the year progresses and the child matures and develops new strategies, teachers can help them move this whole-body, visceral reaction down into smaller toys. A small basket of 4-inch figures of "fighting people" or dinosaurs can be given to a child at a small table where someone who needs to can sit and "fight." This is a safe way for children to play out aggression, or feelings of impotence or anger without upsetting other children. Moving the behavior down to the hands is a way to accept and manage negative behavior, but it cannot be done until the child has developed an ability to think and play in an abstract way (in his head). Unlike younger children who play in a whole body way and seem to "become" the toy, older child can transfer the play to an object in their hands.

Figure 4.2 shows the cycle the teacher initiates.

Talking to the Class about Challenging Behavior

All the other children are watching and noticing how the teacher responds to a child who is out of control. They have all been out of control themselves, and they are all trying their best to be good and big; you are showing them what teachers do when behavior falls apart. If you can remain calm, you will be teaching them you are not upset or afraid of their big feelings and that you are really going to be there for them. Remember, this child is not being "bad" or "naughty," he or she is out of control and needs your help. Some children are embarrassed to become so dysregulated in front of others. If children gather around to see what is going on, that is okay. Use your calming voice to say "Katie is so upset; she is really mad. I'm trying to help her so she can calm down and talk to me. Sometimes getting a drink of water can help; Jay, would you like to get her a cup of water? You can put it on the table and we'll see if she is ready for a drink."

After the child calms down you can talk about this incident with all the other children and the child. You might invite them to sit on the rug with you for a minute to debrief. You can start by saying, "Oh Katie was so loud and mad; she was kicking and yelling and crying—I hope that doesn't happen again! No one likes to get mad like that, do they? Soon she'll remember to stop a moment when she feels the upset coming so she can tell us what she needs." Then you can ask the other children what helps them when they get mad and cry. Some want to play alone, re-center, refresh, and try again. Others need a hug, some a drink of water, some to pound playdough. This conversation builds community in your class and moves the children toward thinking of themselves as part of a group—a group where everyone cares about and supports each other, knowing each child's needs will be met.

Children with Atypical Behavior

Emotional Dysregulation

It is not uncommon for 4- and 5-year-old children to cry now and then, especially in the first days of school, but if it becomes a chronic behavior for a child the teacher may need to make an individualized plan to address it. Crying can trigger many feelings in adults, but the basic goal for the child is the same as it is for any out-of-control behavior—to help the child learn about what makes it happen and make another plan. Generally children don't want to cry, but become so overwhelmed that they can't organize their thinking to respond verbally; it often comes from feeling powerless or afraid. The child will need the teacher's help to learn more effective ways to communicate sadness, frustration, fears and anger.

The teacher can provide the child language for his feelings and discuss what happened after he stopped crying. The teacher helps children use words to move these sad or mad feelings, just like aggressive feelings, out of the lower brain into the upper brain where the experience can be analyzed, processed and controlled. Telling a child to "stop crying," might work with an older child but will not help the young child learn to regulate feelings and emotions.

CRYING AS A LEARNED BEHAVIOR

Some children have learned to cry to get what they want, and need help to understand that what works at home will not work at school. Signs of a learned behavior:

- the child keeps looking at others to see their reactions to his crying,
- the child can instantly "turn it off" if the desired goal is achieved,
- crying seems to go on longer than necessary.

In that case, the best response from a teacher is to sympathetically give the child a quiet place to sit until the crying stops, saying, "I can't help you when you are crying. When you are done crying, I'll come and talk to you," and walk away. Remember that the child is stuck in a strategy that worked in the past, and can be frustrated that it is not working in your classroom, so there may be a period of testing that needs to happen. Stay calm and detached from the drama, but be alert so you can come back and listen as soon as the crying stops.

Once the child has calmed down, review what happened and how he might deal with it in the future. If another child is involved, it is time to bring her over and help the two of them to talk about what happened. Often, there was a misunderstanding, such as "I didn't know you were still using that toy," or "I don't like it when you …" The conversation does not need to end in an apology! Apologies are only appropriate when one child is really distressed or sorry about what happened. Usually the teacher ends the conversation saying something like, "You made a mistake," or "Next time you'll remember to …"

CHRONIC CRYING

If you are dealing with a child who cries often without much obvious reason, you can try several things to help the child learn self-regulation. Having a special place to go to when one is feeling sad can sometimes help; the teacher can ask if there is a favorite book or a special stuffed animal he would like to have there as well. A child may want to bring something from home to keep in the cubby for comfort —Mom or Dad's old sweater, or a lovey. The child might bring a laminated photo of his family to keep in his pocket. Some children may cry from over-stimulation or being over-tired, so a quiet time in the afternoon is recommended for the first few weeks or months of school; some teachers use yoga to help everyone center. If none of these strategies seems to be helping after several weeks, it may be time to meet with the child's parents to explore what else might be going on.

Developmental Differences

Children who are developing in an atypical way may have developed challenging behaviors which help them both cope and compensate for delays. It will take time for the teacher to learn what her reasonable expectations should be for such a child, but she will begin as she does with all children by looking at the individual through the framework of development. While the child's behavior could manifest as that of a child several years younger, the teacher will be setting individual learning goals for her like she does for every child in her class—the goals may just start earlier on the developmental continuum than those for the rest of the class. Children who don't feel cherished and safe in their world may act tough and jaded, manifesting overly mature behavior, or may act babyish and needy. Children with neurological challenges may exhibit a completely different set of behaviors, from an inability to process information and communicate, to behavior problems caused by a lack of impulse control.

In some cases the child will be unable to conform to the needs of the group, presenting a real challenge to the teacher's ability to teach and manage the group. It may be the first time that parents become fully aware that their child needs special support, so there is a time delay as the teacher first assesses the situation in the classroom, then meets with parents to ask for their agreement to seek additional resources, then makes referrals to appropriate support within the district or to outside agencies. Meanwhile, the teacher will do the best she can in her disrupted classroom, and to support the parents who may be grappling with a devastating experience. It is not uncommon for school districts and treatment programs to have waiting lists, making the process of getting the child the help needed take quite some time.

Of course the parents will always love the essence of their child regardless of the child's needs, and want the teacher to see and value that part of their child as well. The opportunity to get to know these children brings wonderful opportunities into the social and emotional growth of all the children in the class and also helps children understand the importance of social justice and inclusion. The teacher will often say things like "You know, Shana just doesn't understand about that yet; she's still learning. We're all learning something new all the time, aren't we?" Teachers strategize about ways to manage challenging behaviors while waiting to get the professional help they need for the struggling children. Using play-alone areas, classroom buddies, and assigning special jobs to both helpers and those being helped can create a real spirit of cooperation and caring in the classroom. A picture chart of the daily schedule and procedures in the classroom can be very helpful to both the child with special needs and the other children, as can a flip chart with pictures of activities to choose from at choosing times. Usually, a child with special needs simply stretches the boundaries of many children's needs, so inclusive practices commonly benefit many children in the room.

Children with serious developmental, emotional, social or physical challenges may profit from sets of special toys the teacher creates just for them. Children who have been exposed to trauma may not feel safe with strangers and might need a private place to get used to the idea of school and being in close proximity to other children. Engaging the child in activities particularly aligned to his needs and interests is one way to get time to teach the group. It also gives the other children a chance to work together without interruption by someone who is not on the same developmental level. Some activities are successful for nearly all children: playdough, like sensory play, is soothing and helps children stay calm. Keep a plastic bag of it ready to offer to the child who needs it in a protected place. A dish tub, kept handy with a few toys in it and a plastic apron, can be quickly filled with water to engage disruptive children and calm them. If water is likely to get out of control use cornmeal with some cars and scoops and toilet paper rolls. A small basket of "fidget toys" can also be calming. Your humane care for all the children will teach the children to also treat others humanely. Be creative; there are no rules for these situations, and your insights, ideas and leadership will make the difference for the children.

Reflection on Chapter 4

1. Adults (parents in particular, but also teachers) tend to respond to challenging or out-of-control behavior in children the way their own parents or teachers responded to them when they were children. Think back on how you were "disciplined" when you were very small (before first grade).
   How did it make you feel? _____
   _____
   _____

   What did you learn from that experience? _____
   _____
   _____

2. Are any of the methods of teaching self-control described in this chapter new to you? Check any that apply:
   ☐ Positive Redirection
   ☐ Observation/parent conference to discover the cause of the behavior
   ☐ Progressive discipline
   ☐ Holding the teacher's hand

☐ Choosing for the child
☐ Making a behavior plan with the child
☐ Other _____

3. Thinking of your current class, are there any children whom you have noticed that need help learning self-control? What methods might be helpful to these children? You can use the chart in Table 4.1 to organize your thinking.

Table 4.1 Planning to support the development of self-control

Name of Child	Challenge for this Child	Method(s) to Try

Chapter 5

Language that Supports Young Children

Key Information in this Chapter

- Using language to build healthy relationships
- Specific language to use with young children
- Increasing vocabulary and interest in using language

The teacher wants his students to feel safe in his care, which will make them relaxed and open to learning new things. Children hearing positive, constructive communication will not only feel the teacher's compassion and kindness, but will also behave more kindly and with more trust towards the other children. He keeps his language positive and constructive, so the children will trust him and come to him for help, and so they will internalize this positive and constructive language and use it themselves. The teacher's thoughtful words towards even those children who bring extra challenges to the classroom will be adopted by the other children, creating a classroom culture of respect for each child regardless of challenges or abilities. Even when the teacher is not there to help, the children will carry his helpful attitude, adopt his language, and continue to help those who need it. This tone and attitude toward others establishes an ambience of community safety, creating room to foster a love of learning in the classroom.

Along with teaching children about the words themselves, the teacher is also teaching them that what they say and how they say it makes a difference. He uses an even, kind tone and avoids adult innuendo, sarcasm, or tones of judgment that can make children feel confused and unsure of themselves. He steps close to the child he is speaking to rather than calling across the room, because language is learned through imitation and he wants children to know that there is no need to yell in his classroom. Lack of language leaves children lacking power (hitting, biting, swearing all stem from lack of expressive language). It is no wonder that children learn and use the most powerful words first (NO! Mine! Go away! Swear words, too, carry considerable power and do not require specific meaning so are simple to use.)

On the most practical level, the teacher speaks to children with kindness and respect because it builds the children's positive self-concept, and people who feel good about themselves are much more able to focus on learning, making the teacher's job more satisfying. A positive self-concept helps the child align his behavior with that of a "good boy," just as a negative self-concept can make a child think "What's the use of trying? I'm just no good." When parents and teachers alike take pleasure in the child's authentic self it feeds that self-concept. In parenting we call this unconditional love, understanding and acceptance … and of course acceptance does not preclude guidance.

The teacher, as a professional without the intense emotional connection of parents, is more objective and intentional in the way he expresses his acceptance and caring, and attends to his nonverbal communication as well. Language is so much more than saying words; as one quickly draws a word up out of the recesses of the mind, he is simultaneously deciding if it is appropriate to the emotional tone of the situation, adapting the volume, inference, and inflection of delivery, and considering the cultural and social innuendo and the receptivity on the part of the person being spoken to. Much of the communication of young children, both expressive and receptive, is nonverbal. The body language, tone of voice, and volume which accompany the words emphasize their meaning. A person can put a soft hand on a child's shoulder and ask "What were you thinking?" in a gentle, supportive tone while trying to understand a child's actions and clarify a problem … or demand "WHAT were you THINKING?" in an angry, judgmental voice which tells the child in no uncertain terms that she had no excuse for making a mistake. The words are the same yet the message is quite different, and the child feeling the adult's support is likely to learn more from the interaction than the one who was made to feel inadequate.

Crystal Clear Language

A clever teacher tells the children what she wants them to do rather than what they should not do. Teacher language tends to be directive, telling children what to do, which elicits obedience rather than self-direction:

- "Move over a little."
- "Wash your hands and use lots of soap."
- "Put your things away, we are going outside now."

This is helpful to toddlers, but does not support the teacher's goal for 4s and 5s to build internal control and decision-making. An alternative is to give simple information and allow the child to decide for himself what to do. When a child is given *information* rather than a *directive*, she will be more likely to comply and experience *self-direction, agency, and responsibility over her own behavior*: in other words the child will be doing her own thinking in response to the additional information that the teacher provides.

- "Where is a good place for you to sit, by me or by Rory?"
- "Looks like your hands have paint on them."
- "We are picking up the toys so we will have room for everyone to sit down. Soon it will be story time."
- "You could ask Jimmy if you can play. I wonder what he might say? Sometimes kids say 'yes' and sometimes 'no'. That's how kids are, you can ask and see."

Here are more examples of information-giving statements. These statements contain advice and suggestions:

- "If you keep your toy near you, other children will know you are using it."
- "When rain boots are on the back porch it is easy to find them when we go out."
- "Your ring would be hard to find if it came off while you are digging in the sand."
- "Before you touch someone else's toy it's always good to ask if it's okay. They might not want you to use it."

You can set a limit in the same information-giving way:

1 "Puzzles are for the table; they get all mixed up if they get on the floor."
2 "Gates aren't strong enough to swing on."
3 "You can cry if you want, but mostly it's mommies who care a lot about crying; other children don't usually care much about crying."

"Need" and "just" are limiting words which can trigger a negative response, just like "No" or "Don't." Rather than say "Just take two" you can say "Take one for each hand." Avoid putting yourself into the middle of a request, as in "I need you to …" Rather, say "It's time to …" or "You need to …"

Avoid vaguely defined words like "good" or "nice" (or "bad" or "not nice"). Be as specific as possible about what is required: "give him a turn," "touch him gently," "listen to her words," "make room for her," etc.

Honest and complete explanations are part of positive speech, and pave the way to trust. Children learn that the teacher has a good reason for whatever she requires of them. Not surprisingly, children begin to speak to each other as the teacher speaks to them. Both children and adults benefit by attending to what they say and how they say it. As one practices being a sensitive presence, a human connection occurs and there is a sense that "we have met and we understand each other."

Anticipating "Teachable Moments"

Children in the primary grades are intuitive and responsive. They often glean more information from your manner, tone, and body language than the actual words you say, so keep a neutral tone and facial expression when you speak to children so they can focus on your language. They need to feel their own feelings without having them affected by your reaction. By 4½ or 5, children are becoming self-conscious; sometimes the most effective correction is a whisper or another subtle correction like making eye contact and tilting your head towards the place he should be. The teacher's goal is to be sure the child knows that the teacher is there to help him learn appropriate behavior, and that adults know that children want to be successful.

1. **When Someone is Upset**

    The teacher can help the child find a private place to calm down and then come back to talk about what happened after the child has regained his composure. Sometimes other children are curious and gather to watch the teacher and child; this can be a very powerful lesson for the watching children if you keep your focus and your heart on helping the struggling child work through the difficult situation. You can narrate the story: "JonJon is so sad he is crying. He is already good at getting his pee pee in the potty but he was so busy that he waited too long to get to the potty, and the button on his pants was hard to undo and now his pants are wet—and he is mad and sad and worried that Granny will be mad. Isn't that too bad that happened! He'll remember not to wait so long next time, right?" The teacher's intent is to help the child understand himself, normalize the situation for others, and supply constructive language that helps the child identify and talk about his big feelings. The language she supplies will move the experience out of the reactive brain that has him crying and upset and not thinking about how the whole situation developed, and moves it into his logical brain where it can help him work it out and prevent it from happening again. (See also Talking to the Class in Chapter 4.)

2. **Giving Directions**

    A child may not know how to carry out a request that seems obvious to you. "Hang up your jacket" may not give the child enough information; saying "Here is your hook and here is the little loop the tag makes on your jacket; put the loop on the hook and it won't fall down," provides detailed information. "See how we put the blocks away, square ones here and rectangles next, then long half rectangles, then longest of all here. When you put them back like that you'll always know where to find the size you want when you are building." Telling the children "Put your hands on your lap," helps give the children information about how you want them to sit so they will have the most success sitting on the rug with the rest of the group.

3. **Sharing Ideas**

    Be as transparent as possible about what you are thinking and doing. There is no reason to surprise or confuse children, and they will appreciate being respected enough to be included in what you are thinking. "I'm going to ask a few children to get up from circle and begin getting the classroom ready for us before circle is quite over. Listen for your name and see if I ask you. Those of us who are still on the rug will read one more silly poem." This message reminds the children that everyone has their own needs and all needs are being met here; nobody is being favored for arbitrary reasons. This helps children avoid judging and comparing what they do with what others do, and worrying that others are getting something that they are not. The children learn that you are reasonable, in charge, and thinking flexibly to help everyone get what he needs.

4   **Modeling Acceptance**

The teacher watches for opportunities to promote an atmosphere of acceptance in the room, reminding children that we all do the best we can and everyone has some things that are easy for them and other things that are harder. "Kyra is a great block builder and Glory is very good at making letters, and Kyra is working on letters and Glory is working on building. That's how people are; that's just right because we are all learning."

5   **Responding to Questions**

When children ask questions, be sure you understand the real question before you answer. When in doubt, ask. Remember the old joke about the child who asked his mother where he came from—she responds with a long description of human reproduction only to have the child say, "That's interesting, but Jimmy said he came from Oakland and I just wanted to know where I came from." It is always good to take a minute to be clear about what the child is wondering. You can say, "It sounds like you are thinking about babies" (or whatever) and "What has got you wondering about that?" Taking cues from the child, you will be able to more closely meet the child's need. If the subject is inappropriate or too large and confusing it is best to say "That's an interesting idea" and drop it. Later, if you choose to, you can come back to the subject to correct information. This way you can help the child understand without making him feel foolish or shamed. Often children don't need a lot of details. If they ask where babies come from and you think they don't need a biology lesson you can say something like babies come from their mommy's tummy. If the child continues to ask the same question it is often a clue that you are answering the wrong question.

Whenever you are unsure about how to respond to a child's question, it never hurts to answer by repeating back what he has said. This will give you time to think as well as a chance to see what he is thinking or wondering. Following up the question with clarifying questions before you answer will help your answer be more appropriate. You can always come back and bring up the subject again if you feel uncomfortable with an outcome. "I was thinking about what happened yesterday; maybe I misunderstood, maybe you were thinking about ..."

Remember that young children are relatively inexperienced with language and may need to hear the same thing many times before they pay attention. Repeat the same information several times until the child absorbs the message if you feel the child needs that (beware of falling into nagging, though, as that teaches children not to listen). Sometimes if a child is having trouble understanding it helps to use body language—patting the chair as you say, "Here is a chair for you to sit in when you are doing a puzzle."

Socially Acceptable Language

Teachers model, extend language and build polite language. This builds the child's social skills, as speaking to another child or adult in a friendly manner is more likely to have a positive result. Words like "Please," "Thank you," and "You're welcome" are all best taught through hearing the adults frequently model their use in appropriate situations—not just when speaking to the children, but also among adult interchanges.

When children try out profanity they may be looking for a reaction from the adults or their friends. Most young children do not know what those words mean, but do know their effect on others and the situations in which they hear them used. The best way to defuse this behavior is to make it boring for the child by not responding emotionally to what is said. In a matter-of-fact voice simply say, "Oh you better not say those words—grown-ups really don't like it when kids say them. Grown-ups think children who say those words are not nice children. You are a good, kind, friendly person so it is best not to say those words around grown-ups so they don't get mixed up and get mad at you." If the child persists, you may say "It seems like you really need to say those words right now. You know I don't like to hear them so (if your classroom has a bathroom) you can go into the bathroom and say them where I won't hear them, then come out and play when you are done." Other children will take their cue from the teacher's unemotional reaction and soon go on with what they are doing. If your classroom does not have its own bathroom, you might designate an out-of-the-way corner where the child can say those words to himself until he is ready to come back and play.

Useful Phrases for the Classroom

Positive Speech

By saying "You can do it this way" instead of "Don't do it like that" (by avoiding "don't") the teacher avoids any suggestion that the child is doing something foolish, being inadequate or clumsy, or making a mistake, and supports the child's self-esteem. Often young, intuitive learners only hear the last words you say, so "don't throw the sand" becomes "throw the sand." Or the child hears "OK" when someone says "That's not OK." Communication is clearest when children hear what you do want them to do. It is a kindness, for in truth they often do not know what to do and you will discover that your suggestion will likely be more helpful than what they can think up. You might say with regard to throwing sand (or a rock) "Where is your bucket?" or "I wonder if there is room for a new rock in our rock collection in the science area?" (Soon you'll have everyone clearing the yard of rocks; you may need to use a wastebasket to hold so many, or paint them and decorate the classroom, weigh them, or count and measure with them.) Most importantly, in the big picture, the children can see that your goal is to enhance their experience at school rather than limit it.

Part 1: Words for Teachers to Say to Children

"Walking feet" or "Keep your feet on the floor." This is classic positive speech. "Don't run" becomes "Walking feet," "Don't stand on the chair" becomes "Keep your feet on the floor," "Don't yell" is "Talk to me in a friendly way." Tell the child what you do want her to do so she can both stop the unwanted behavior and be clear about what you want her to do next.

"Tell me about ..." your drawing, your painting, your building, your digging. Children live in present time and often paint, draw, dig, or build just because it is interesting but without planning for any particular final product. They are enjoying the process of creating in the flow of ideas, so often don't have an answer to a question like "What are you making?" A child might begin to make a rainbow but accidentally draw a circle instead, and then decide to draw lots of circles, and then decide to fill them in and make polka dots ... We want children to know that we value this flow of imagination and creative exploration, rather than requiring an end goal, so we ask instead to be included in the process with "Tell me about." It won't be long before they learn to value the end product and will be eager to tell you what they made.

"I don't know what you want when you say 'No.' Tell me what you do want." It is easy for children to get into the habit of saying "No." It is a powerful, controlling word, and also a dead end. Once you've said "No" there is nowhere to go, so helping children tell you what they do want rather than what they don't want can avoid getting stuck in a power struggle. Asking the child to tell you what he wants means that he is much more likely to do it, if you agree, than he would be to do what you suggest. If a child is in the habit of saying no, every option you offer may just elicit the word "no" over and over again. Asking the child to name what he does want breaks the cycle; with younger children, though, you may need to limit options by asking "Do you want this or that?" In addition, you are helping the child to build a habit of positive speech—rather than telling people no, he is learning to say what he wants.

"Tell me when you are ready." This comment gives the child time while continuing to hold her to the agenda at hand—of course, the dilemma for the children is that while we are happy to wait until they are ready, they are not allowed to do anything else but get on with the adult's agenda. The words are "Oh, I see you'd like to go look at a book [or whatever] now; as soon as you are ready to put away the puzzle [clean up, put your jacket on, etc.] you can go do that. Are you ready? No? Okay, I'll wait; you can tell me when you are ready." Whatever the child wants to do that is not what the teacher wants her to do can be done as soon as she completes the required task; otherwise we can wait together. Soon the child will realize that some tasks are simply required, and it is more effective for her to comply because the refusal interferes with her freedom to move on. This works best during playtime. If you need everyone to come to the rug and someone refuses to join the group you can say "Too bad; we'll miss you at story" and ignore the child. Sit so the child can't see what you are showing or doing, but you can watch her with your peripheral vision; usually the child will complete the task and join the circle, so have a spot ready that you can pat for her to sit on when she joins, then continue with your agenda without comment.

"It is a little tricky." Many things are a bit tricky for a child! Tying shoes (or untying a knot), starting a zipper, forming letters, squeezing just a drop of glue—the day is full of challenges. We use this phrase to help children know that we know it is not simple or easy, but we have faith that with some persistence and practice they can achieve their goals. Identifying the task as something to work on can help the children know they might have to be creative and try different solutions before they will succeed. We want children to work on it, and we want them to know that even though it might not be easy we trust that they can do it.

"That's fancy!" We use this to describe something with a lot going on; people can be fancy, as can ideas, clothes, artwork, and even a complicated block building. Children can feel quite proud of themselves for being able to do something "fancy" and being acknowledged for a difficult or complicated task.

"You really worked hard on that!" or ***"You look very proud of that!"*** Children often ask adults to admire something they have produced; this is a useful phrase to acknowledge not the product but the work that went into it or the way the child feels about it. These phrases remind the children that their own feelings about their work are more important than adult praise. Sometimes it is appropriate, too, to say "You look disappointed about that. Tell me what happened."

"It looks like your hands need some washing." This phrase avoids giving a direct order, which often elicits resistance. Instead, phrase the order as an observation or suggestion. When "go wash your hands" is changed to "it looks like your hands need some washing" the child is less likely to resist. "Put your jacket on" can become "I wonder where your jacket is?" Prompting the child to look for his jacket plants the idea that he needs it before he goes outside, and allows him to take care of this himself without feeling micro-managed.

"Everybody is different and everybody is learning." One of the goals for PreK and Kindergarten children is that they learn about themselves; we want every child to feel that he or she is just right for being him or herself. No one is perfect and no one is expected to be just like anyone else. We are all learning and trying our best, and everybody will do what they do in their own special way. We want children to feel safe reaching out and trying hard things, and not to judge others or themselves harshly. This builds resiliency and a strong sense of self, as well as acceptance of others' differences.

"That was a mistake" or "Oh dear, there was a mix-up." Whenever children do something wrong, even if we know that they "know better," we frame the event as a mistake or a mix-up. Everyone does get mixed up now and then and make a mistake, but ultimately we know the child is good and wants to please. We also know that it is easy for the reactions of the primitive brain to override the judgment of the neo-cortex when children are upset, making self-control extremely challenging for the young child even though she "knows better." Even what looks intentional really was a mistake driven by the lower brain—the mistake was in not being able to get hold of the upper brain in time. We want to reinforce the child's sense of self as a good person who can do better so we keep the focus on the positive, and that mistakes can be corrected and mix-ups sorted out.

"I won't let you hurt anyone." There is a basic agreement that children need to feel safe in the classroom, and the children need to know that the teacher will protect them both from others and from their own immature impulses. It is perfectly appropriate for a child to be upset and tell people how he feels, but the teacher is going to remove a child from a situation if he uses physical aggression of any kind.

"I'm going to help you choose now." The ultimate punishment for a competent 4- or 5-year-old is the loss of the privilege to choose and do what you want to do when everyone else is allowed to. When children are out of control, over-excited, hurting another child, or destroying another child's work, the teacher will help the child calm down and center herself so she can come back into control. The teacher starts by suggesting that the child needs the teacher to choose for her: "Better sit down and find something quiet to do so you can go back and play some more. Would you like a book or a puzzle?" or "I see room for you to play in the sink here with the boats." If this doesn't calm the child, a moment to sit close to the teacher and take some big breaths might help. If all else fails, the child will have to hold the teacher's hand and walk around with her as she teaches; this sends a clear message to the child that "self-control is the price of freedom," a key life lesson. See Challenging Behavior in Chapter 4.

"Oh darn, that just didn't work, did it? Next time you'll remember ..." This is the way a teacher commiserates with a child who is living with the consequences of being unable to control himself. A child who keeps throwing sand, after a reminder that it needs to stay low, may cry as if his heart is broken when he is barred from the sandbox. The teacher may give a hug or empathetic pat and say "Oh phooey, you'd like to play in the sand but I just can't let you throw it. Next time you'll remember to keep the sand down, won't you?" Along with the sympathy comes the teacher's confidence that the child is learning and will do better next time.

"If you want to spit you can spit in the toilet [or wastebasket]." This goes hand in hand with "If you need to shoot you can put your finger through the fence and shoot there." The goal is to allow the unwanted behavior yet make it so uninteresting that the child will choose to stop doing it. Standing by the toilet spitting is not much fun so usually the spitting ends quickly; shooting also loses its excitement if you are standing at the fence shooting at no one, and not getting a reaction from anyone. Be creative; this technique works with lots of different kinds of limits.

"I wonder what you were thinking about?" This is a good question to ask when you need to buy some time and formulate your response. When a child asks a surprising question you can clarify and check about what the child is thinking by asking the child to explain further.

"You can't make other people do things, but you can always decide that you want to go do something else." If Child A is playing with Child B and Child C joins the play, Child A might decide he would now rather play with Child C yet continue the same activity. He starts telling Child B to go away. Children can always decide to go off with another child and play somewhere else, but they can't just kick people out of the game because the options changed. This response helps the children keep the play friendly instead of saying things like go away, you can't play, I got it first, or I made up the game. We say "You can't make other people do things; they decide for themselves just like you do. You can choose to go away and play somewhere else if you don't want to play here, but you can't choose for other people."

"Here you are at school. Things are a little different from home here, (or your old school, etc.) aren't they?" This is an orienting statement to remind the child that he is in a new and different place so he needs to notice what he is doing and pay attention to others, remembering we have different rules. This reminds children that the playground is not the park or the back yard, and the classroom with all the children is not a birthday party. This comment can start many conversations, for example: "Here you are at school. Things are a little different from home at school, aren't they? At home parents might change their minds if they hear crying, but at school children are not likely to change their minds because of crying. It's better to talk to them about what you want, because they understand words more than crying. You can say 'You were too close to my blocks!!'"

Part 2: Words to Teach Children to Say to Each Other

"I'm using it now; you can use it later." Before a child can share with generosity he must experience ownership, so when children are first learning to play together the rule is that an item is yours until you are done. When you are done and put the

toy back or leave the area, then someone else gets a turn to own it. Each child knows that no one is going to ask them to be done with a toy until they finish playing with it. We want the children to know that we value and respect what they are learning and doing, and do not feel it would be kind or respectful to insist that they give away something they are working with and enjoying. (You wouldn't like someone to take a book you are reading away from you and say you had to share it!) On the other hand, we also want the children to communicate with each other and to respect others' wishes too—they will be encouraged to let the other child know when they are finished and it is his or her turn now.

"I get to choose for myself." Teachers coach children to say this when another child is trying to tell them what to do. Choosing is a privilege given out of respect for the children's ability to be responsible for themselves. When children can choose they are much more likely to engage in the activity or toy, and to work harder at solving the problems that come up in the activity. Of course there are times the teacher does not allow anyone a choice, such as coming in from the yard. Children who feel empowered may try this line on the teacher, who can respond "Yes, you get to choose at playtime but now it's time for me to choose." Teachers encourage children to choose but take away that privilege by choosing for the child if the child is not managing to make acceptable choices.

"I'm just playing with _____ now; I will play with you later." We want children to learn to play successfully with a friend, and if including a third or fourth child in the play is too challenging for the social skill level the teacher protects the twosome. It is hard work to be in a big group of children all day long, and sometimes playing alone or with just one friend is what one needs. If another child comes and asks to join two children who are busy with their own agenda, it is okay to tell the other child (in a friendly voice) that he is busy now with a game for two but will be happy to play with him later.

Techniques for Promoting Language Development

Children learn language best by practicing it throughout their daily activities, whether they are learning a first or second language. Teachers should encourage children to talk about what they are doing, and respond to their meaning with genuine questions or remarks. When children make grammatical errors it is more helpful for them to hear the correct model used in speech by another child or an adult than to hear a correction. (Child: "I hadded to walk to school." Teacher: "Oh, you had to walk today? Who did you walk with?") The more children use language—especially with feedback from adults—the faster their language will develop. In the primary grades a silent classroom is not an optimal learning environment; the more a child uses and practices language the better he becomes at speaking. It is difficult to be truly literate until the language is mastered in speech.

Many teachers are familiar with and concerned by the "30 million word gap" identified by Dr. Betty Hart and Dr. Todd R. Risley and studied since the 1960s. In 2003 they found that children at the age of three in various socio-economic circumstances had vastly different levels of exposure to language: the average child growing up in poverty was exposed to 616 words per hour, working class children heard 1,251 words per hour and children born to professionals heard 2,153 words per hour. Over the course of the first three years, the children born to professionals heard 30 million more words than those born in poverty. Those limited vocabularies carry terrible implications for future learning.

When children learn to read, they skip over words they do not know but can glean meaning from the context of the sentence by using the vocabulary words they do know. Then, the words they have learned through context become part of their vocabulary the next time they come across them. Those with a larger vocabulary can more easily learn through context than those with a more limited vocabulary. As sentences become more complex, the gap grows because the children have more and more trouble deciphering sentences, while their classmates have thousands more words in their vocabulary to fill out sentences and construct meaning. These vast differences in vocabulary have a profound effect on fourth grade reading level.

The more conversation your classroom supports, the more vocabulary and meaning the children acquire. The more you extend their thinking with your adult words and your adult ideas, the more they expand their thinking. Children (and some adults) love words, making up special secret words for just such a jump or the special way the sand feels, or how we think a word might sound when spoken in another language. This is all good, as it trains the ear to hear differences in sounds as the child begins to sound out a word, discerning the difference between "shock" and "shark" or "flute" and "fruit." Nursery rhymes, poetry, nonsense poems, and finger plays all teach and encourage auditory discrimination, and build the vocabulary necessary for success in reading and literacy.

Relying heavily on nonverbal communication, young children and second language learners shrug, point, push, smile, or break eye contact as forms of communication. Children need to know that words work for them by helping them get what they want, knowing what others are asking of them, and communicating not only what they want but how they feel, what they think and what they wonder about. Children need to realize that words have meaning that deepens and broadens relationships. Catherine Snow and Connie Juel, in their book *The Science of Reading* (2005), note that vocabulary drills and flash cards diminish the meaning of words, while play increases meaning and understanding. Talking, listening, and imagining with children helps them find the symbolic meaning in everything; pictures stand for objects, just as marks in the sand can be letters standing for a sound. Playfulness is particularly suited to language learning, as is expression in all forms; singing, painting, dancing, and drawing all promote communication, literacy and the development of language.

Stimulating Language Use in the Classroom

Vocabulary and Grammar

Vocabulary is learned as the teacher talks to the child in the context of whatever the child is engaged in. A new word needs to be heard in different contexts over many repetitions before children begin to use the word in their own speech. Here are some ways to develop vocabulary throughout the day:

1. Expansion: Repeat what the child said in adult form:
   Child: "Truck go."
   Adult: "Yes, your truck is going."
2. Extension: Respond to the child's meaning and encourage further conversation:
   Child: "Truck go."
   Adult: "Yes, your truck is going. Where is it going?" or "I see your truck is going somewhere and carrying a lot of blocks."
3. Questions: The number of questions that children ask correlates with their language development.
   a. *Respond with interest to what children ask you or tell you.*
   b. *Model questioning by asking them questions that call for complex answers (not "What color is the dog" but "Why do you think the dog was running away?").*
4. Model complex language:
   a. "The sky is so beautiful, with all those shades of gray as far as the eye can see."
   b. In the story, Annie wore her red dress and called her dress crimson. If you are wearing crimson shoes today, you can go wash hands for lunch.
5. Speak to children as if they were adults rather than correct what they say directly, which may inhibit talking:
   Child: "No want shoes on."
   Adult: "I see you don't want to put your shoes on."
6. Be alert for "gaps" in children's vocabulary. When you see a child pointing to an object rather than naming it, or hear a child misusing a word, that is the word you need to teach. Teach it by using it in conversation with the child, repeating it several times, such as:
   Child: points to a purse in the playhouse, or calls it "that thing."
   Adult: "I see you need a purse. What will you put in your purse?" etc.

Quiet Children

Quiet children can become invisible in the group, and need special adult attention. These children need to learn to speak up, ask for what they need, and defend their positions. Children who are silent, watching and following, may be trying to understand their new role as a student, while other children have no trouble

Figure 5.1 Playing alone and playing in community are equally valuable skills
Source: Photo courtesy of Monaire Taylor.

speaking up and expressing themselves but do need a little longer to process and think about what is going on. Some quiet children just need practice getting the words out, some are unsure about how to react when the other child's words come at them. Some children do not talk because they are anxious about making a mistake, being interfered with, or judged. Others have a developmental speech issue that requires professional intervention. Again, the first step for the teacher is to make a point of observing to try to gain insight to the reason behind the quietness. Then she can look for opportunities to create and support conversational experiences for them as she does for all the children.

If the quiet child seems to be self-sufficient and competent, he may not need your help with suggesting appropriate language—he may just be the kind of child who only speaks when he feels he has something important to say. He may need you to sometimes remind the others to wait a minute to hear what he has to say; soon, he will be able to say by himself "Wait a minute, I want to say something." Others may seem lost and need your help; often those children will turn a pleading look at the teacher when they feel stuck. The teacher can supply words then, "Jack, you can say 'Thanks, I like my drawing just like this, I don't want to change it'" (or 'I want a turn being Daddy, I have a new baby at my house, you know'). Standing nearby as he speaks may be enough help, while other times the teacher will need to both supply words and offer to hold his hand while he speaks to the others, saying, "Here, I'll help you tell them." Thoughtful adult guidance, positive language and a happy class atmosphere can allow the child to start seeing himself as a competent communicator. Just practicing what to say in positive, socially acceptable ways can help. Once a child is on the radar the teacher will begin to know when to help; you might decide to let him be the big billy goat in the class show, or to dismiss him first into the dollhouse, or have him choose the story and tell the class why he likes it. Guided play provides a unique teaching opportunity to help a temperamentally quiet child learn to speak up, just as it provides opportunity to help the overbearing child learn to step back.

Children's Literature is Rich in Vocabulary

Books are a rich source of academic vocabulary for young children. Be aware that different books are written for different purposes. "Easy-Reader" books, or other stories with limited vocabulary, are great for 5- and 6-year-olds to practice what they already know about reading, but not helpful in enlarging children's vocabularies. Children's literature uses a richer vocabulary and needs to be read aloud to children many times, so they can get the sound and rhythm of beautiful language in their ears. Choose different books for different purposes: predictable books for the children to chime in for the chorus, counting books where you want the children to count with you, and so on. However, books with beautiful illustrations and a rich vocabulary are to be listened to and enjoyed. Illustrations in a high quality picture book offer both aesthetic pleasure and are also an integral part of telling the story. Younger children with more limited vocabulary and listening skills rely on the illustrations to carry them through the story; older children can be carried more by the language alone. Be sure to read one or two vocabulary-rich books every day that are appropriate to the children's listening skills.

At the beginning of the year, you have taught the children to listen to a story without interrupting, especially to a new book. Of course, you will want to begin with short stories, so children who are not used to listening can succeed at staying quiet. The teacher models this by not interrupting himself the first time he reads a new book, stepping out of the way so the author can speak directly to the children without commentary. (If you think children will not understand the story without your help, you can pre-teach one or two of the important words before reading the story. If there are too many new words, save the book for later in the year.)

For the purpose of expanding children's vocabulary, choose books with interesting words. After the first reading, you can answer questions or make explanations to help the children understand the story. On later readings of the same book—because you will want to read a worthwhile book many times—the children will already know the story and will not be thrown off when you pause to talk about a word or ask children to describe what is happening in the picture. Rich books can lead to rich conversations!

There may be a few words or phrases in a book that really capture the children's imagination. Four-year-olds love to say long, grown-up words, and 5s will pick them up even more quickly. Using new words in everyday conversation will really embed them in the children's minds. Children learn language through imitation, so if the teacher uses a word or phrase often, children will pick it up. Some examples are:

- A teacher who has read Mother Goose poems to the class may say, "One shoe off and one shoe on, diddle, diddle, dumpling, my son John" as she ties shoes, which infuses what could be a silent exchange into a playful encounter.
- Another teacher noticed that children responded to the word "concocting" in *Chicken Soup with Rice*. Later that day he asked the children in the playhouse, "What are you concocting in that pot?" The teacher's goal was both to teach the word "concocting" and to stimulate children's interest and curiosity about words.
- A Kindergarten teacher might write two or three interesting words from a book on a post-it where he will see it, to remind him to use that word in casual conversation with the children during that week. Sometimes, waiting in line for a bell to ring can be a good time for these short conversations.

Choosing Good Read-Aloud Books

Notice which books the children like; most children like stories with rhymes, and they often like stories that have a refrain ("Run, run, as fast as you can—you can't catch me, I'm the gingerbread man!"). The children eagerly anticipate the refrain and are excited to recite it with you. Most children at the PreK/K age like books about things they know about, with younger ones liking stories about real things that might really happen to them and older ones liking real things that happen out in the world.

A good children's librarian is a valuable resource, as she has really seen which books are popular with the children, and can always help if you need a book on a particular topic. Look for stories about things the children are wondering about: how the dog next door had puppies, how the post office gets letters to Grandma, or what happens at swimming lessons. Books about feelings can be helpful and create an opening to discuss situations that come up at school, building understanding of emotions and creating empathy (but remember that teaching about feelings is best done in the moment rather than in the abstract). Just as the best teaching at this age is subtle and hidden within the curriculum, the best morals are delivered through stories about real people doing real things. Counting books and alphabet books are also interesting. Use discretion with fairy and folk tales, as well as Halloween tales, that could be scary. Young children can become very upset by thinking about vampires or ogres as they are still developmentally fuzzy about what is real and what is pretend.

Language that Supports Young Children 155

Figure 5.2 A love of books, not ability to read, is the goal of early childhood
Source: Photo courtesy of Geraldine Rocha.

Books teach, so be sure you are teaching what you want in the stories you read (it is okay to decline to read a princess or superhero book a child brings to school, saying "Thanks for bringing that, but I already planned to read some other books today.") Notice if pretend stories deliver real meaning for children; a story like this can be a sort of filler rather than a teaching tool, so read the books to yourself first so you can decide if they are what you want the children to hear. Stories should be clear and help children understand and organize the world around them. (You need to know what a walnut shell is before you can understand that a princess can't really keep her clothes in one.) As you introduce stories about make-believe and pretend, look for stories in which the pretend ideas have a sort of logic or reason; this way the story itself can scaffold the child's understanding into fantasy stories and extend and build the imagination. Now and then, some PreK/K favorites are nonsense stories or stories with a sense of humor—but beware, while sometimes they are just the thing to get the sillies out, at other times they may stimulate them!

Age-Appropriate Poetry and Stories for Young Children

Teachers begin reading books with pictures to help the child keep their focus on the story. The pictures communicate the story, so sentence length can be short and the storyline uncomplicated. As sentences get longer and more complex, the pictures become smaller and less important than the words to hold the storyline. Besides picture books, teachers should read short poems to children from time to time. Listening to the words without a picture to look at teaches children to visualize and also to pay more attention to the *words* rather than the picture. Also, poets use words in interesting ways, which promotes symbolic thinking.

A poem for 4-year-olds

THE PROUD CAT
There was a little cat
Who wore a yellow hat
And a fine fur coat all of yellow.
He had a white tie,
And he held his head high
Because he was a proud little fellow.

– *Edith H. Newlin*

(This poem is short, with only two new vocabulary words (proud and fellow). All children are familiar with cats, making this an easy poem for them to visualize. Being "proud" of yourself is an important concept for 4-year-olds.)

A poem for 5-year-olds

JUMP OR JIGGLE
Frogs jump
Caterpillars hump
   Worms wiggle
   Bugs jiggle
Rabbits hop
Horses clop
   Snakes slide
   Sea gulls glide
Mice creep
Deer leap
   Puppies bounce
   Kitten pounce
Lions stalk—
But—
I walk!

– *Evelyn Beyer*

(This is a longer poem, with many rhyming words. It also has rich vocabulary and interesting ways to move. Fives will be able to act it out, once they learn what the words mean. It can also be extended to practice creating new rhymes—an important skill for 5-year-olds.)

A poem for 6-year-olds

THE FOLK WHO LIVE IN BACKWARD TOWN
The folk who live in Backward town
Are inside out and upside down.
They wear their hats inside their heads
And go to sleep beneath their beds.
They only eat the apple peeling
And take their walks across the ceiling.

– *Mary Ann Hoberman*

(This poem has more abstract concepts that 6-year-olds can appreciate. It can be extended by asking children to draw what Backward town might look like. It is especially good for 6s, because they have a well-developed sense of humor, and enjoy silly rhymes and stories.)

Finger Plays

A quick finger play or a song is a good way to bring the group together. When children gather on the rug they are likely to want to chat with each other; if the teacher launches into a song or finger play as the children gather it serves the purpose of connecting everyone without conversation. Children are likely to want to be part of the group so if they are dawdling on their way they will quickly finish up whatever they are doing and hurry to the rug. Once the need to connect has been addressed, the teacher can move on to more direct instruction. Some children do not like to participate at first, but if they are allowed to watch they will soon want to be part of the activity. They are still learning quite a bit through imitation so they almost cannot stop themselves from participating. You may hear from a parent that the child who has never said a word in the group all year sings and recites finger plays all the way home! In songs or circle time activities, always ask the child's permission and see if they want you to sing their name or if they are willing to "fly over yonder" or "get under the hat;" if they say no they don't want to, go right on to the next child. It is always okay to opt out, and allowing the option will ultimately increase the child's interest in participating.

Here is one to start with; ask long-time teachers to help you grow your repertoire.

> **My Turtle**
>
> *Hold out your fist with your thumb tucked inside your fingers—pat your fist*
>
> This is my turtle.
> This is her shell.
> She likes her shell,
> Very well.
> She pokes out her head when she wants to eat.
> (pull your thumb out from inside your fist keeping your fingers curled tight)
> Wiggle your thumb as the "turtle" eats
> And pulls it in when she goes to sleep.
>
> *Pull your thumb back into your fist.*

Putting on Shows

Five-year-olds also enjoy acting out stories. Any story will do, but start with something like *The Three Billy Goats Gruff* in which the roles are small and clear, and with a strong structure (a clear beginning, middle, and end). Read the story several times, then suggest to the children that they might like to put on a play of the story.

Brainstorm what is needed to put on a play and make a list for reference—actors, costumes, a director, a stage, seating for the audience, ushers, etc. Help the children choose who they want to be and let them make their costumes of tape and paper. Suggest some make a stage; others can get chairs for the audience and make tickets to sell. Some might like to be the pre-show band. This is another way to inspire a lot of talking, planning, and structuring; sometimes the show never happens because the planning is so important. Remember that is okay, because the organizational thinking and talking is what is the most important. Children who opt out might like to come back and be an audience, and children who are not able to play the role they want can be reassured that there will be another turn on another day. If it really comes to pass, the class next door can be invited to come and watch as well.

Reflection on Chapter 5

1. Our habits of speaking are usually unconscious and automatic. We no longer listen to ourselves, especially in difficult situations. To break this pattern and notice how we are speaking to children, we may need to take a step back and ask ourselves these questions. Again, think back to your earliest memories.
    - How did my parents speak to me when I did something they didn't like?
    - What tone of voice was used when they were proud of me?
    - If they were calling me, could I tell from their tone of voice whether it would be good news or bad news?
    - Do I hear an echo of my parents, other family members, or teachers when I am talking to the children? What would I like to hear?

2. Look over the list of "Useful Phrases for the Classroom" and choose three phrases that you would like to start using. Write them here, and then tape them up where you will notice them when you are teaching.

    _____
    _____

3. How much talking do the children in your classroom use on a daily basis? What do they talk about? On a relatively quiet day during playtime, eavesdrop on some of their conversations. (If there is never a "quiet day," then put a tape recorder near the playhouse or the playdough table, and listen to it later.)

    While you are listening notice and jot down ideas for ways to make that conversation a "teachable moment": New vocabulary words?

Questions to stimulate more conversation? Correcting any misconceptions you noticed? Modeling a more polite way to say something?

Of course the teacher can't hear everything children say, but taking some time to analyze where your students are in their language development will make you more aware of how much you can enrich their language with casual comments as you go through your day.

Chapter 6

The Bridge from Play to Instruction, and Instruction to Play

Key Information in this Chapter

- Effective use of play-based and direct instruction, and how the two modes complement each other
- How to learn the children's needs through observation of their play
- Best groupings—whole-class groups or small groups—for various activities
- How to teach a small group while other children are engaged in self-initiated play

Typical child development includes some surprises; a big one is that children learn to be part of a group (conforming with the teacher's plans) because they first feel seen as individuals (through the experience of choosing for themselves). We have talked about the continuum in learning development, beginning with the majority of learning coming through play and individualized interventions, and moving towards greater capacity for direct instruction. The 4-year-old year begins heavily focused on the play end because the children still see their own needs as paramount. Gradually, as the children feel seen as individuals, and are ready to be part of the community, and develop the brain–eye–hand maturity needed for reading and writing, the classroom includes more instruction and less play.

As is true in all areas of growth and skill development, there is a long transitional period while the child integrates new abilities. A baby does not just stand up and walk; for weeks and months he stands, falls, stands, falls, takes a step, falls, etc.—and even after he can walk across the room, for some period of time may continue choosing to crawl most of the time. The older 4-year-old or 5-year-old can succeed in overcoming his egocentric needs and being part of a group for small periods of time, but retains the need to choose for himself sometimes as well. Knowing that the choosing and playing allow the child to relax and re-center, the teacher of young children plans a day that allows each child time to periodically retreat and recharge through play—freely chosen, self-structured and self-directed. This will give him the energy and enthusiasm he needs to join into class activities again later.

This chapter demonstrates how to introduce small pieces of instruction in meaningful ways, first in the context of the children's play and then more for its own sake.

Emergent Curriculum

Direct Instruction and Emergent Curriculum land on opposite ends of the teaching spectrum, and both are essential tools when working with young children. Even the youngest child is able to accept a small bit of instruction here and there—think of the toddler trying to climb a new slide who is happy to have his teacher suggest "Put your hands here and your foot there." But that toddler is not going to learn much by listening to someone describe how to climb. There is no reason to use only one tool without the other; however, most teachers are only trained in one method and therefore view it as "the way." Emergent Curriculum is a teaching system that uses both methods in partnership. Giving children time to work in an emergent learning environment is particularly helpful as the group learns to work together at the start of the school year, when new students join the class, and when helping young children learn to regulate their feelings and emotions and develop social skills. It provides a natural way for the teacher to help the children build relationships, and for the teacher to get a sense of the child's learning readiness. The open structure of the Emergent Curriculum gives the teacher the opportunity to individualize learning and help the children who have not had positive experiences outside of the home or in groups. These children will need the open classroom experience as well as direct instruction by the teacher. Regardless of the children's skill and experience level, the Emergent Curriculum can also be used by the teacher to see what they understand from the lesson, to practice incorporating new information, and to expand their vocabulary while the children stabilize and strengthen their learning experience.

The term Emergent Curriculum describes an individualized curriculum and the evolution of group themes that surface through the children's school experience. The teacher's role is to prepare the classroom to entice exploration and inspire conversation among the children. The teacher sets up a constructive environment with materials and equipment that young children typically enjoy. The children are given support to explore and experiment with their understanding of the world around them and their understanding of who they are in the world. Conversation in the playhouse area will soon allow the teacher to see family dynamics, communication and vocabulary skills as well as pre-reading, writing and math and science concepts as they engage with the materials. The teacher's presence creates safety, offers coaching and social skills and sets a learning ambience for the children's learning. Along with creating the set up the teacher studies the children to watch for ways to extend the children's learning experience. As she observes what the children do and say she is ready with ideas to extend their understanding of how the world works. Emergent Curriculum should grow and change with children's interests, with the growth and evolution of the group, and with the input of new ideas supplied by the curriculum as well as the teacher.

Observing and Extending the Play

The teacher discovers what children are thinking about by observing and listening to their freeflow conversations. As the teacher learns the children's interests she can add supplies to the play area to extend the child's thinking and develop the complexity of the play. Alberto and Johnny often build roads in the block area. Traffic signs can be added to the block area to extend road-building (and introduce the literacy concept of a sign communicating important messages to drivers), then arches to create bridges, construction trucks to support the road-building and boats to sail under the bridges. As a larger group of children become interested in this play, group themes emerge; the teacher adds a map with icons of local landmarks to the wall in the construction area, and soon the children may be drawing their own maps of the roads and construction plans. Using the Emergent Curriculum model, the teacher adds books about roads, pictures, building plans, and measuring tapes to the classroom. The teacher's alignment with the children's interests, and her ability to feed information and subtle suggestions to the builders, creates the themes and extends the building. Emergent Curriculum is like playing leapfrog with the children's minds—first the teacher is following their lead, then she jumps in front and adds new ideas, then she falls behind again to see how they incorporate those ideas, then she jumps in front again with another play suggestion that will align the children's play interests with her learning goals.

Observing play is both an active and quiet activity on the teacher's part. This interactive observation occurs in the play areas with the children, as they are dependent on the teacher's presence to help them manage their behavior and support their budding social skills; it cannot be done from behind a desk. Children who have a tenuous grasp on self-regulation have better success managing their behavior when they know they can trust the teacher to be there to help if they get in over their heads. The teacher has thoughts about the direction the learning may go so she is watching for opportunities to help the children; at the same time she knows that she will learn the most about the children if she allows the children to lead the direction of the play as long as it remains safe and constructive. Staying close and listening to ongoing conversations gives the teacher the opening to extend and expand the child's thinking by adding information or asking a question. Flexibility is paramount for both children and teacher as the flow of play allows ideas to move and shift; as the box car turns into a shark tank the teacher may need to facilitate with a new idea to help expand and keep the play positive.

Along with watching play, themes emerge through listening to the children's language as they play. One teacher heard several girls talking about the shots they had to get before enrolling in school, so she set up a small doctor's office near the house area with a blanket on the floor for the cot, medical props, a clipboard, and some chairs for the "waiting room." This theme was enriched by reading books about doctors, nurses, and other community helpers at story time, and asking the children what other items they might need for their doctor's office—which the teacher listed on chart paper to include a meaningful literacy experience.

Sometimes themes last several weeks and sometimes just a day. The teacher is attuned to the play so she can tell when a theme is winding down and it is time to make room for a new interest. Because the children's experiences are limited, the teacher plays an important role in expanding their thinking. The combination of what each individual child brings to the classroom, the evolution of individuals into a group, and the teacher's subtle guidance bring the Emergent Curriculum alive through the complementary opportunity for the children to play about what they are learning.

Here is another opportunity for the kind of documentation described in the section of Chapter 1 called "Explaining Learning in Play to Parents and Colleagues." Emergent themes that involve many children can be displayed on a bulletin board for parents and visitors; photos of the children playing in that area along with their artwork on the topic are good visuals. Some days the teacher might write down the children's words about their discoveries in that area as well. Teachers can also display the way the play supports other areas of learning; for example, after the children measured all the different sizes of blocks in the block area the teacher helped them make a chart that displayed how this play developed their math concepts.

Individualizing the Curriculum

Not everyone in the class is interested in busy group areas like the blocks or the doctor's office, so the thoughtful teacher adds a quiet corner that may interest a quieter child. It may be some live insects or snails or growing plants in the science center, or a place for only two children at a time to experiment with blowing soap bubbles. She watches for opportunities to extend this interest, too. She may give children new vocabulary about what they are interested in, or she may ask a leading question such as, "I wonder what would happen if ..." to turn their play in a new direction.

The teacher is able to do all this because she has carefully set up the classroom in areas that suggest developmentally appropriate play. The children can succeed and be self-sufficient with as little adult direction as possible during playtime, leaving the teacher free to move through the children's play observing, guiding and extending each child's work. As the year progresses the teacher adds to the equipment in each play area so it will evolve and expand according to the needs and interests of the children and the goals of the teacher. In this way the teacher builds the curriculum through the environment.

Seasonal Themes

Along with this environmental structure and Emergent Curriculum, a seasonal theme guides and runs through the curriculum. The annual changes of the seasons inform the choices the teacher makes for the group, the focus activities, and the themes of the art projects. For example, spring brings dirt to explore in the sensory table, pastel colors at the art easel, and animal families in the matching games on the manipulative shelves. Gluing projects of cotton balls and pastel cupcake papers on pale blue reflects the spring sky, and focused science activities carry the seasonal theme of planting seeds. Stories on the bookshelf also reflect the springtime theme.

Following annual seasonal themes harmonizes the children's school experience with what they are experiencing in their daily lives. Winter, summer, and fall bring similarly thought-out themes. The seasonal themes reflect an appreciation for the rhythms which move life. The anticipation of winter holidays is balanced with the inward sleepy quality of winter, and the outward reach of springtime brings the anticipation of a quiet lazy summer. These rhythms build the human condition and are honored in the teacher's curriculum development because they help the children feel part of and understand the world around them.

The more experience a teacher has with Emergent Curriculum, the more she will be able to think of ways to deliver content within play-based settings. Once the children trust the teacher to give them time to pursue their own ideas, the teacher will find she has more latitude to lead in the "leapfrog" game. By establishing a strong play-based curriculum in the first months of the year, especially with children who are not yet 5 years old, the children will become ready for more teacher direction in the last half of the year.

Blending Academic Instruction with the Emergent Curriculum

The philosophy of an Emergent Curriculum honors all the learning that happens while children are trying new activities and interacting with their peers. It is important that children be allowed to choose their own activities during this part of the day—remembering that "true play" is freely chosen, self-structured, and self-directed.

The standards of the Early Childhood Rating Scale (ECERS) require that self-initiated play be available to children for "a substantial part of the day," at least a third of the time that children are in school. "Recess" is not counted as part of that time unless it happens in an "outdoor classroom" with opportunities to engage in activities that are as complex as those offered in the classroom, with the same caliber of teacher guidance available. Many academic skills can be woven into these free choice times by providing literacy and numeracy materials. Some things that can be added to centers are:

- clipboards and pencils for writing in the dramatic play area
- alphabet and numeral puzzles
- letter and number cookie cutters for playdough
- blank "books" (stapled papers) and word/picture cards in the writing center

The Bridge from Play to Instruction   165

- manipulatives that let children practice matching shapes and putting objects in order and create sets as they sort by attributes
- patterns turn up as children string beads and paint pictures
- a book about street signs near the block building area encourages children to make signs and label their constructions
- small toys (or felt board characters) that follow the storyline of a picture book along with the book—for the children to act out the story
- board books in the house area encourage children playing mommy or daddy to read to the baby dolls
- Making tickets, or money for the store, gives numbers additional value
- Making lists and charts, measuring, and sending notes all support academic development.

These give children opportunities to practice and review things that have already been taught in direct instruction. It is effective because children choose what they are interested in working on. Children will usually spend more time working on activities that they have chosen for themselves than one that is assigned—in fact, adults are also much more inclined to work hard at something they choose for themselves! Children will explore the ideas in different ways. Some children will try and try to do things in some ways that don't work before they hit on the one that does. Although this may seem like an inefficient way to learn, it is not: when

Figure 6.1 A spontaneous invitation to the Dance Party!
Source: Photo courtesy of Monaire Taylor.

understanding comes through the child's own reasoning and experimentation it is more likely to be internalized, and less likely to be forgotten. Teachers are there to answer questions or to suggest a different approach by saying, "I wonder what would happen if ..." and setting the child off on a new experiment. Sometimes a child will choose the same ABC puzzle or counting game several days in a row, as they internalize their own learning. (See H.J. Freiberg and A. Driscoll, 2005, *Universal Teaching Strategies* as cited in Developmentally Appropriate Curriculum, Fifth Edition, Pearson 2011.)

At free choice time set out activities that make the children think: a good example of an intrinsic academic learning tool is a puzzle that has five dots on one piece and the number five on the partner piece requires that the child count the dots to find the match. An ice cube tray with a different colored dot in each square and a variety of objects in matching colors can offer opportunities to sort through and think about attributes and matching, as well as identifying color names. The teacher, casually stopping by, can comment "Oh, I see you've put all the pink pieces in one hole and the magenta pieces in another hole" if the child needs a little vocabulary input.

Some children need to play out social situations with dramatic play materials, some like to use small dollhouse-type people, others like small cars and still others relate to small plastic animals. While not academic in the traditional way, giving children these opportunities and materials to work out fears and social confusion and social power dynamics will open up their capacity to take in more academic knowledge. A worried brain does not learn nearly as well as a relaxed brain.

Group Instruction

In Chapter 1 we described the components that add up to self-control, one of the strongest predictors of success. A major goal for this transitional age is that the children learn to be intrinsically motivated to manage their own behavior. This is the motivation that comes from within the children and supports the children's capacity to know themselves, take responsibility for themselves and be able to care appropriately for their own needs while being kind to others. After this foundational understanding of oneself is established, the child is much more able to learn to conform and respond appropriately to adult direction of a group. The developmental sequence begins with the child knowing and understanding himself, then moves to honoring his own competence and independence, and finally moves to his making a choice to conform for the greater good. The child must be given time to learn "me" before he can learn about "we."

At some time between the ages of 5 to 7 years children begin to be more interested in being part of a group; their egocentric thinking decreases, and they have both the **will** and the **skill** to become part of the group. This is the point when extrinsic motivation—motivation from outside oneself—will not interfere with their developing sense of self. Extrinsic motivation is adult direction and control done for the good of the group rather than intrinsic motivation, which focuses on teaching the individual child and meeting the individual child's needs. When a child is struggling, the chances are that he needs individual attention. It helps that child to hear the teacher acknowledge his need for individual attention even when she cannot give it to him at that moment in the midst of the busy classroom. Saying something like "I hear your voice getting loud, and I see that you wish I could help you right now. As soon as I finish with this group I'll come right over," lets the child feel seen and heard by the teacher. Offering to let the child hold your hand while you carry on with what you are doing also can help, and so will giving a moment of individual attention before it is asked for. This need for attention indicates immaturity, and should pass in a few months if the child has an opportunity to build a positive relationship with the teacher.

In many elementary schools, some of the day is spent in strongly managed time such as assemblies, preps, eating lunch, resting, and lining up for transitions. This means that the teacher-directed academic time needs to be both *powerful* and *age-appropriate* in order to be effective. As you think about the flow of the children's day be sure you balance active activities with quiet ones; exciting activities need to gradually ramp down to restful activities so the children can integrate what they

Figure 6.2 Children ready for small periods of group instruction
Source: Photo courtesy of Monaire Taylor.

have learned. Fours and 5s are learning to balance their energy output and they are trying hard to be good as they experience a new and challenging classroom experience. They will be more successful in class if the daily schedule supports their need to recharge their batteries with down times to look at books and do puzzles as well as times to practice following directions or negotiating with other children. Teachers help children learn how to balance their day by creating a balanced daily schedule. It not only helps the children, it helps the teacher who doesn't have to work with over-stimulated and over-tired children.

Powerful direct instruction for 4s and 5s is both *short* and *interactive*. Most children can be fully attentive listening in a group for about 3 minutes per year of age. (Of course, this is an average—attention spans vary with temperament and experience.) That means that at the beginning of the 4-year-old year, you can count on about 10–12 minutes of whole-group instruction at one sitting—stretching out to 15 or more minutes at a time by the end of the year. However, there is no rule that says you can only do this once a day! Three short group times of 10 minutes each are far more powerful than one 30-minute session. To make the most of these short windows of opportunity, the teacher must be super-prepared, with all materials at the ready before the lesson begins.

Whole groups are best when they are used to:

- give mini-lessons that *everyone* needs (letters and sounds, introducing theme concepts)
- read a story or a poem and talk about it as a group
- singing, finger plays, daily announcements
- build community within the classroom.

Small group instruction can be both more *interactive* and more *powerful* than whole group. In a small group, everyone can have manipulatives and receive individual attention from the teacher. *(For management suggestions for small groups, see the next section, Flexible Grouping.)*

Small groups (3–5 children) work best when they are used to:

- provide intervention to children who need extra support
- group children together who all need the same skill
- involve a hands-on activity such as a bingo game, counting cubes, or pencil and paper practice
- are fairly short (5–15 minutes).

Effective Whole-Group Instruction

Before you begin a group discussion have the children sit in a circle where they can all see each other, and have a small ball that can roll across the rug. Seat children strategically; separate friends, and put children who get silly or are shy near you so you can help them easily. The teacher rolls the ball to a child and only the child with the ball talks; when she is done speaking that child rolls it to another child.

Here are some ideas for topics that are age-appropriate for young 5-year-olds in a large group:

- **Building reflection and self-awareness:** Talk about getting along with others. This should be mostly the children talking, with the teacher asking questions to guide the discussion she would like the children to have. "How do you know someone is your friend? What do friends do? What could you do so they know you like them too?" Toward the end of the year, as written words become more important, the teacher can chart the children's ideas, read it back to them, and post it for parents to see.
- **Learning about each other:** "What do you like to build in the block area? What do you like to do in the yard? What book do you like best? What do you do when you are mad? What do you like others to do to help you if you are sad?" Again, as the children coalesce into a group that enjoys these conversations for a longer period of time, favorite activities can be graphed for the group as a math project as well.
- **Talking about a problem that occurred in the classroom:** "How did you feel when _____ happened? What can you do when you are unhappy or scared? How can we help someone who is upset? What do you think we can do the next time this happens?"

Group discussions should be short, not more than about 10 minutes (that is a long time to wait for those who are not participating). If the teacher is doing most of the talking that is a sign that the discussion should be abandoned; the teacher can develop some new strategies for facilitating the children's discussion and try again another day.

Through the intrinsic motivation of the children to succeed in their play, the children learn to moderate their own behavior. In Kindergarten and first grade children will be able to see themselves as part of a group, but as 4-year-olds many are still challenged by this. Ultimately, they learn that there is great pleasure in working with others for the success of the group, and that is what will ensure their success in an elementary school classroom. After knowing themselves and the needs and desires of the others around them, we can trust the developmental social drive to push children to step back and make room for others' ideas in order to maintain harmony and participate in the pleasure of group activities.

Flexible Grouping in the Elementary School Classroom

Imagine an engaged classroom of children who are busy choosing their own activities and settling down to play. The humming rhythm of children learning, playing and getting along fills the room as they talk and work things out together. From her desk the teacher sees three children moving pieces on the felt board while they retell the story of the Three Billie Goats Gruff in the book area. Another group of children are working with Legos; lying on the rug, stretched out and chatting, they build cars and spaceships and a landing base. At one table a girl is building a zoo with small plastic animals and some small table blocks. She goes over to the writing center to get some masking tape so she can mark the borders of the zoo. Children sit around another table drawing, cutting, and pasting as they chat and help each other with letters and phonetic words they are adding to their artwork. Three of the older children are playing BINGO at another table, while keeping one eye on what the rest of the group is doing. A child at the puzzle table goes to get a friend to come help with the tricky part. At the playdough table six children are rolling playdough "snakes" and forming them into letters and making words. The dramatic play area and the blocks are closed at this time to encourage a quieter playtime during this "modified play" period that is described at the end of Chapter 3. The teacher is at her desk giving a private lesson to three children beside her. She is watching the children in the classroom as she meets with her little group. Today she has gathered children who need help with letter recognition; she has made up a game for these three who are sorting and matching the letters, making piles of those that match. She has picked three children who are all working on the same learning challenges; by sitting with them in a small group the teacher can help them catch up to the level of the other children. After about 10 minutes the teacher compliments them on their work and sends them back to the group play. The teacher stands up and walks through the classroom of playing children, making supportive suggestion to extend the children's learning as she pauses at one cluster after another. She may admire their constructions, help to facilitate interpersonal challenges, or suggest that a child is ready for a different activity. After a few minutes of making sure the big group has what it needs, she will be ready to gather up another little group of children and return with them to her desk for another private lesson.

Most teachers do not have time to meet with each student one-on-one to meet their individual needs, yet no two children are exactly alike. The way teachers with a large number of children and little adult assistance solve this problem is by making their intervention groups very flexible. The flexible grouping system used by the teacher above looks deceptively simple, but that is because the teacher has worked hard to be sure the children know how to play with the equipment available, and has organized her room very carefully to support independent play, before she started pulling out small groups. This preparation cannot be overemphasized; without it the teacher will never be able to keep her focus on an intervention group.

How to Introduce Small Group Time

1   Do not begin small groups until your students have mastered the routines of choosing and ending activities independently (refer back to "Assembling the 3 Rs—Room, Routines and Relationships")! This may take a while ... in the meantime, get to know your students and teach them strategies for solving their own problems and getting along with others. A younger group will start small groups much later in the year than an older one. The more independent they are, the better small group time will be.
2   Begin slowly, by limiting the afternoon playtime to "Independent Centers" for the first week or so. The teacher will not pull groups, but will observe all the children using the centers and debrief the process every day, giving them feedback on how they can become more independent and solve problems without the teacher's help. As she is building trust with the children, it is important that these discussions stay non-judgmental—discussing behavior that was not helpful to the play and coming up with ideas that do work, rather than blaming or shaming anyone for making social mistakes. "Everyone is learning and everyone is growing" is the teacher's mantra when children tattle on others' misdeeds.
3   If the teacher is lucky enough to have one or more assistants in the room at this time, whether paid or volunteer, she makes sure the other adults in the room understand her routines and goals for play so that they will be consistent and effective in their support to the children.
4   When the teacher observes that students are managing independently for 15 minutes or more, the class is ready for her to begin to work with a small group. Continue to debrief the class on how they are handling themselves as necessary, and allow plenty of time to observe and circulate around the independent play areas between pulling small groups.
5   As the children's stamina for constructive, independent play increases, more groups can be called. Teacher's observation of the whole class informs what happens next. If children begin to have problems playing without her facilitation, the teacher may have to go back to observing the class and debriefing until focus improves, when she can start pulling groups again.

Flexible Grouping System Example

The details of the system outlined below may seem daunting at first, but after a little practice the teacher will find it an enormous help in keeping her classroom humming and learning.

The chart in Table 6.1 of student assessment data shows the differing needs of ten children in a combination classroom of PreK and Kindergarten, children aged 4 years 9 months through 5 years 11 months, in an elementary school where the teacher has 25 children on her own. This age group in an early childhood setting

Table 6.1 Planning for individualized intervention groups

Child	Letters and sounds	Counting with 1:1 correspondence	Fine motor/ handwriting	Phonemic awareness (K only)
PreK				
Annie	Need	Need	Need	
Bert	✓	Need	✓	
Felipe	Need	✓	Need	
Graciela	Need	Need	Need	
Kindergarten				
Cody	Need	✓	✓	Need
Dartrice	✓	✓	✓	✓
Ephraim	Need	✓	✓	Need
Henry	✓	Need	✓	✓
Imogene	Need	✓	✓	Need
Julieta	✓	✓	✓	✓

Need indicates a need for intervention in the area.
✓ indicates child is on track for this time of year.

would be more likely to have multiple teachers. The columns on the chart could change for an older age group or as the year progresses as goals are achieved and new ones are set.

There are several ways to form groups to give each child what she needs:

1. Form one intervention group for each skill needed.
    - Annie and Graciela qualify for three intervention groups.
        ○ Letters and Sounds—first the teacher will offer activities like that described in the scenario at the beginning of this section, where she simply gives the children opportunities to study letters and see what distinguishes one from another. After they can easily distinguish a "b" from a "d" she will move on to a game of placing objects on the letter of the alphabet corresponding to the initial sounds of their names.
        Counting with 1:1 Correspondence—in each session children will be provided with sets of small objects with a matching set of "holes"— 12 plastic eggs and an egg carton, 12 counting bears and a muffin tin, pegs and a pegboard, etc. Children will count one number as they place each object into a hole.
        Fine motor/handwriting—those children who need intervention in both this area and letters/sounds will not be included in this group

until they make progress on recognizing letters, as it makes no sense to ask children to write letters until they understand their differences. The first activities when children are pulled out for this group will be coloring with long slender crayons, with the teacher gently assisting children to develop a tripod grip and making sure the children write their names on their papers (they do not have to be legible).

Knowing that the children form the foundations for these focused activities through repeated play experiences, the teacher makes these materials regularly available in the classroom for the children to explore—either as stand-alone activities on the manipulative shelf or embedded in the play areas (e.g., eggs in a carton in the dollhouse). See additional suggestions for small focus group activities at the end of this chapter.

- Dartrice and Julieta will not be in any group.
- Most children will only be in one or two groups.
- Notice that one Kindergarten student (Henry) will be in the counting group, because he is missing that skill while all the other Kindergarten children have mastered it.
- As some children master a skill before others, those children can leave the group sooner. The children who need more time will stay longer as the group gets smaller.

2 Make smaller groups by focusing on fewer skills at one time.
- For example, break the Letters and Sounds group into two groups of three children each, so there is more participation. Choose children with the same needs or who work together well in forming the groups.
- Smaller groups may be of shorter duration or meet less often, as they are a more powerful intervention than larger groups.

3 Prioritize which skills will be taught first, to make it manageable.
- To help with classroom management, choose one or two skills on the chart to teach first. For example, a teacher may decide to begin with just the K students, or to begin with just the most basic skills, such as counting with 1:1 correspondence.
- Depending on the class and the time of year, a teacher may be able to teach only one intervention group during a period, or perhaps as many as three. (See how to start groups, below.)
- Not every group needs to meet every day. An intensive group may meet daily, but most groups only need to meet two or three times a week.

4 Consider each child's overall development.
- Annie and Graciela each have several needs. Pulling them out of their center time every day defeats the purpose of the interventions, as these children probably would also benefit from experience with their peers in

the play centers. Again, prioritize their needs so that they work on fewer skills at once and still have time to participate in class activities.
- Dartrice and Julieta—and probably others—are right on track in every area. Still, the teacher occasionally calls an enrichment group with a special activity for these capable children. This group does not need to meet very often, but an occasional meeting both normalizes the small groups, showing that every child has a turn, and keeps Dartrice and Julieta from feeling left out because of their competence.

5 Tips for keeping the groups effective.
- Continue to reassess (during small group time) and change groups every few weeks. Children's needs are moving targets. Children can be added to or dropped from a group as their needs change.
- Be prepared (have materials ready before calling children) and keep it short: 10–15 minutes is a good time for a small group lesson.
- In between calling each intervention group, the teacher should plan 5–10 minutes to walk around the room to check on how children are doing at their independent centers. A little attention to their needs will help keep them on task while you work with the next group.
- Keep it flexible! Some days a teacher might call two groups, other days only one, depending on the time of year and the maturity of the children. Often small group time begins very slowly and increases as the year goes on.

For a reminder about how the other children remain occupied while she works with small groups, see the section in Chapter 3, "Modified Play to Support Academics."

Activities for Small Groups with the Teacher

PHONEMIC AWARENESS

- Read a short rhyming book and ask students to tell you which words rhyme, then help them think of more rhyming words with the same rhyming pattern.
- Use flash cards with pictures only, say the word aloud, and ask students what the first sound is, then have them repeat the sound.
- Make a list of things they can think of that start with the sound /k/. A scaffold for this is to have small toys or pictures of things that start with /k/ and other sounds.
- For Kindergarteners, say some CVC words (cat, pin, red, etc.—words spelled with a consonant–vowel–consonant pattern) and help the children say all three sounds they hear. A scaffold for this is to model how to do this first and have the children repeat the teacher model.

The Bridge from Play to Instruction 175

LETTERS NAMES

- Tracing sand paper letter with finger
- Draw over letters with tracing paper
- Make letters out of playdough
- Sort letter shapes into piles
- Make small BINGO cards with only a few letters at a time, using some of the letters they do not yet know. This game can be played over and over, and new letters can be added.
- Have each child name the letters on their name cards. Add last names or some simple sight words when they are ready.

COUNTING WITH 1:1 CORRESPONDENCE

- Make a grid with tape and sort small objects onto the grid, one object per square.
- Read a short counting book and have children take turns counting as they touch each object on the page. Children who can do this without help up to 20 are ready to move to a higher group.
- Use small plastic counters and ask each child in the group to line up a specific number, then count the pieces with them to see if they did it correctly.
- Have children count their steps, or count as they hop or jump from one "x" taped on the floor to another … you can do it too. This is especially suited to kinesthetic learners.

RECOGNIZING NUMERALS

- Play number BINGO up to 10, then to 20.
- For Kindergarteners: Staple together small blank books with only five pages. Have beans or stickers or something else to glue on the pages. On the first page of the book have them trace the numeral 1, then glue only one item to that page. On page 2, the numeral 2 and two items, etc. After the books have been made have the children chorally read them with you as they point to the numeral and then count the items on the page. After they have mastered the first book, make another one from six to ten.
- Give each child a number card and some beans. Can they put the correct number of beans on each numeral? All the children in the group can help each child count the beans to see if they are correct.

FINE MOTOR/HANDWRITING

(Notice physical issues such as dominant hand, grip strength and pressure, and support writing with a tripod grip; teach rules such as ordering letters in a word from left to right, putting space between words.)

- Draw (family, home, dog, suggest details).
- Copy shapes, use stencils.
- Have the children make patterns on the rim of a bowl by attaching different colored plastic clothespins. (Wooden clothespins can be colored with colored markers.) This exercise strengthens finger muscles.
- Have children who need more work with scissors practice by cutting on curved lines, making snowflakes, or cutting a fringe on their paper.

BLENDING/SEGMENTING SOUNDS

(For children over age 5)
- Collect some picture cards or small toys and lay them on the table. Be sure to only use very short words with sounds the children know. Play "Guess My Word." The teacher says the sounds in the word, and children try to guess which car/toy it is. If they guess it correctly, they can take the card or toy. When a child has guessed three words correctly, he "wins" and can leave the table. The group gets smaller until the teacher is only working with the children who need the most help.
- "Cat, bat, hat"—use flip cards where the "at" doesn't change but initial consonant does and help children put the onset-rime (initial sound and ending sound) together.
- Have children dictate stories and you sound out the word as you write, ask for their help with the CVC words.
- Sound BINGO. Use letter cards, but instead of calling out the name of the letter, just call out the sound it makes.

As you go along you will easily make up games and ideas that the children will enjoy; keep a stash of ideas and props like these and use them year after year. It is important that you play with the children as you coach them. Notice what they like and are interested in and incorporate those things in your game—sort matchbox cars when the group loves cars, and kitty cats if the group is into animals. You don't need to go to a lot of expense; children can cut pictures of cars or cats out of old catalogs or magazines, then sort and organize them. You can keep them in an envelope and use the same props again and again.

Flexible Teaching Reaches Every Child

The teacher's toolbox is vastly expanded once she becomes adept at teaching through play and individualizing her instruction for each child. Adding these skills to the classic elementary school teacher's systems for teaching one lesson to the entire class gives her confidence that she can meet each child in her classroom at his developmental level, and find the tools that will support his growth to the next level of learning.

The Bridge from Play to Instruction 177

Figure 6.3 Children enjoy practicing, especially when it is their own choice
Source: Photo courtesy of Geraldine Rocha.

Every teacher worries that allowing children to choose for themselves and initiate play will result in a classroom full of chaos and unmet learning goals. It can help build a vision of success if you visit another classroom—a nearby Kindergarten or a good local preschool—which has an established program based on true self-initiated, self-structured, and self-directed play as a teaching vehicle. It is remarkable and reassuring to see a room full of focused 4-year-olds engaged in multiple play areas, seeming as if they hardly need the teacher. Watching the teacher closely, however, you will also see her subtle support for every child in the classroom. You will see her casually moving around the room, standing close to the group whose play is looking disorganized and asking a focusing question about their plan. You may see her just make eye contact across the room with a child whose voice is rising, then see the child take a breath and tell his playmate, in a friendly voice, what he needs. You hear her reassuring a child at the art table that she will soon be there to help her spell her sister's name on the drawing of her family. You may see her quietly walk to the cupboard and pull out small notepads with pencils attached, then set them on the shelf in the dramatic play area where children are playing restaurant. Seeing this classroom reminds you that the teacher has laid a tremendous amount of groundwork as well; the children all know how to choose, use, and return materials to the shelves. They know how many children may play in a given area, and acceptable uses for the materials in that area (playdough stays on trays, paint goes on paper, puzzles are worked on tables). They trust their teacher to be tuned into their play, to know where they might need support, and to help them when they need it rather than scold them for making mistakes.

You too can be that teacher providing many pathways to the children, with confidence that they all lead toward your learning goals. Children playing with playdough, taking their dolls to the doctor, climbing to the top of the monkey bars to save people from the fire, or pondering over a hard puzzle are all learning how to listen to others, how to share ideas and resources, how to approach and negotiate problems, how to be part of a group and how to take care of themselves.

Your classroom will be the one where every child feels seen and heard and supported. As we learned in Chapter 1, these are the foundations essential to all future academic learning and school success. We know that children with a healthy social and emotional base will have the developmental drive to grow and learn, and also the will and capacity to take in the teacher's contributions to their learning. Learning to teach through the flexible use of play and instruction contributes to the success of every child.

Reflection on Chapter 6

1. This book has focused on matching high-quality instruction with children's brain development and learning styles. In the first box, check suggestions for working with young children that have worked for you. In the second box, check those that you would like to try, or need to keep working on.
   - ☐ ☐ Emergent Curriculum (developing areas of study from the children's interests).
   - ☐ ☐ Extending children's play (taking their ideas in play to another level).
   - ☐ ☐ Individualizing your curriculum (having a variety of choices available so children can follow their varying interests).
   - ☐ ☐ Using whole-group time to build community in your classroom.
   - ☐ ☐ Meeting individual needs with focused, small intervention groups.
2. First look at the ones that have worked for you. Think about why they worked. Had you tried any of them before? Did they fit with your natural teaching style? How will you expand on what you are already doing well, and keep them fresh and exciting? Write your ideas here:

   _____
   _____
   _____

3   Now look at the ones that are still a work in progress, or that you would like to try. What do you need to become more skilled in this area? More practice? More information? A colleague you can brainstorm ideas with? Visiting a program where these things are already in place? Choose one direction that you would like to grow as a teacher and think about the resources you need to make that happen. Write one goal to work on in the coming year, and the steps you will take to achieve it.

_____
_____
_____
_____

Appendix 1

Typical Patterns in Development from Ages Four to Six

Growth is steady and predictable, yet also uneven. Some children are more physically precocious, and some are more verbal. This chart is organized to indicate, on the left, what is typical of an *average* 4-year-old and on the right what is most typical of an *average* 5-year-old—knowing that each *individual* 4- or 5-year-old will be on his own particular trajectory. As noted elsewhere, a child's chronological age may not align with his development. An inexperienced 5-year-old may exhibit some 4-year-old behaviors.

PHYSICAL MOTOR CONTROL	
Younger Behavior	Older Behavior
• Very energetic. Moves at high speed. • Manages all large muscle activities well. • Modulates volume of voice. • Can sit for a prolonged period of time at manual tasks. • Stands on one foot, can break rhythm in stride when running, can climb, jump, and hop. • Awkward in bouncing a ball, can throw overhand. • Hand dominance is still forming in many; stronger tendency for left-handedness or ambidexterity in boys than in girls. • Dances with natural grace in movements; interprets and demonstrates response to rhythms; can gallop and is learning to skip. • Visually focuses on specifics; while able, less likely to use peripheral vision and panoramic view or big picture awareness.	• Coordination stronger, more agile. • More mature sense of balance. Rests head on desk and falls out of chair when in need of physical activities to increase blood circulation. • Excellent postural control and core strength; sits and walks with good posture. • Child easily changes position from standing, sitting, squatting. • Less physically driven to move; stays in one location for long periods when pursuing interests. • Stands on one foot or his toes for several seconds. • Good at handling tools. • Can throw a 5" ball, then catch it using hands more than arms—but looks at partner's face rather than the ball. • Can: jump rope, balance on rails or top of a wall, walk on elevated plank, roller skate, skip in time to music, walk on a line on the floor. • Child is active but can settle.

COGNITIVE DEVELOPMENT

During the ages from 4 to 6 the brain is making a major transition from the egocentricity of babyhood to a more socially based, objective relationship with others. The brain is also shifting from thinking and experiencing everything in a gestalt of life, with the child at the center totally in present time. By the age of 6, the brain is able to sort and categorize information into different topics and is ready for more academic instruction.

At 4 children are still absorbing everything from everything, reacting and responding and collecting more and more data about themselves and the world around them, just beginning to see the value of controlling oneself, anticipating and planning ahead, and doing what one is told. By Kindergarten, children are calmer and have a better understanding of how the world works and how people behave. This is stabilizing and brings that quality to the 5-year-old.

Younger Behavior	*Older Behavior*
• Beginning to think things through with less adult help needed to generalize or guess what might happen.	• Ideas more in focus, thinking processes more precise and decisive.
• Follows simple two or three step directions.	• Finishes what he starts, and remembers from day to day so that he can continue on the same project, though if he loses interest or if things take too long, he will either abandon it or ask for assistance.
• Intuitive reasoning increases. Can pick largest and smallest and can sort and order. Understands most, biggest, and both, but not same or equal.	• Remembers and follows sequence of three or more commands.
• Responds to the total, not parts. More likely to focus on emotions and feelings of others than on words.	• Reality oriented and practical; can tell fact from fiction.
• Excellent memory; knows his birthday, address, phone number, what he had for dinner.	• Thinks in realistic terms with very little abstraction.
• Lives in the present time. Knows morning, afternoon, evening and night.	• Feels he knows everything and will argue if corrected.
• Depends on sequence of routine to know when things will happen, before lunch, after lunch, after pick up.	• Can choose a "medium" size, as well as small and large.
• Uses positional words (center, middle, edge) with vague notion of meaning.	• Learning about weights and money.
• Sees similarities and differences between himself and other children.	• Can follow the plot in a long story and repeat a long sequence.
• Confused about real and pretend; unsure if dinosaurs exist.	• Personifies inanimate objects.
• Thinking is not yet fluid; can get fixated on one idea or plan.	• Lives in the here and now, but has a better sense of time and duration.
• May say, "I don't know" while thinking about something else, not because he doesn't remember or know.	• Most recognize and write numbers up to ten; many able to count to 100 and read numbers up to 20.
• Lacks moral sense; fabrication to serve his own ends or make a story more interesting seems fine.	• Most can write letters and identify their names and some words, and write them.
	• Speech can fool one into thinking he understands more than he does.
	• Beginning to understand weeks and months, if reminded.

LANGUAGE DEVELOPMENT

Younger Behavior

- Talks in a stream of consciousness, unable to hold thoughts in the mind yet. Uses language for attention and social rapport.
- Questioning is common. "How" and "why" questions are frequently asked; often already knows the answer but likes to hear the rephrase.
- Average vocabulary is 1,500 words. Average sentence size is 4.5 words. Sentences are complete and joined with conjunctions.
- Uses more articles and adjectives. Grammar and vocabulary developing rapidly.
- Combines language with all play activities, talking incessantly, as he thinks aloud.
- Listens more intently and finds humor in silly language, nonsense words and plays on words. Picks up cultural phrases, clichés, adverbs, and expletives rapidly.
- Speech becoming more abstract and reflective with more personal and social references.
- Still makes grammatical mistakes and misuses words. Over-regularizes verbs, as in "runned" instead of "ran."
- Verbal restrictions more effective than physical, but not very sensitive to praise or blame.
- Loves rules for others but feels they do not apply to him.
- Conversations are clear and directed as in true dialogue.
- Secondary comprehension. Can understand and answer questions like "Why do we have houses?" and "What do you do when you're hungry?"

Older Behavior

- Uses all the common language patterns of adults, with sentences complete, correct, and finished in structure and form. More complex sentences and conjunctions.
- Average vocabulary is 3,000 words, and words used more accurately.
- Asks fewer questions, but they are more relevant and informational.
- Most can articulate all sounds in first language, with /l/ and /r/ the last sounds to be mastered.
- Voice is still high-pitched, but intonation is more mature.
- Uses practical dialogue and commentary in dramatic play.
- Slang or swearing purely imitative, used to create drama.
- Form of speech is adult, but content is unsophisticated.
- Interested in meaning of words, and using new and large words.
- Asks: "What does _ _ _ spell?"
- Criticizes incorrect grammar in others.
- Can define simple words.
- Begins to use language thoughtfully and evaluatively. Uses phrases like "I think," "I forgot," "that's hard," or "that's easy."
- Language, as well as thinking, is more abstract.

EMOTIONAL CONTROL

The brain growth in 4-year-olds leads to a life-changing leap in the child's sense of self. The child is aware that life is moving him towards higher independence and expectations, which creates a quandary: he knows he is still little and cannot compete, and at the same time wants to be bigger and thus be granted the responsibilities and respect given to older children. This shift requires leaving the comfortable role of a young child totally held in the safety and protection of adults to a much more independent life, lived more in the company of peers. Four-year-olds can find this shift in consciousness scary, which makes them feel and act out of control. They are deliberately challenging as they test to see if they could actually be ready for this change. They work on the skills they will need to succeed by being intentionally challenging and difficult so they will better understand the reactions of others and their role in the interaction.

Sometime after the fifth birthday they complete this testing, and accept and complete the transition leading to a period of calm ... there will be one more round of testing at around age 6 which completes this shift in consciousness.

Younger Behavior	*Older Behavior*
• Fears and worries can be irrational, scaring oneself with one's own imagination.	• Relative homeostasis follows the challenging 4-year-old.
• Confusion about what is real and pretend in fears, dreams, television, movies, computer games, monsters, nightmares, the dark fear of death. All indicate growth in awareness from concrete thinking to more abstract thinking, and increase the child's anxiety level.	• Enjoys group experiences.
• Poised, calm, interested in pleasing the teacher and following rules.
• Sees self as big.
• Occasionally resistant but equanimity prevails even in stressful situations.
• Serious, businesslike, realistic, literal, imperturbable, and excited in anticipation of the future.
• Emotions and feelings are big and out of bounds; exuberance and excitement can quickly swing to quarrels, resistance, arguments, sulking and tears. Bravado, boasting, exaggerations and swagger are coping mechanisms.	• Purposeful, persistent and careful.
• Shows satisfaction in their productions, and pride in their possessions.
• Enjoys his own slapstick humor and jokes he makes up.
• Quarrels between children are less frequent and often settled without help.
• Need supervision; resists firm limits; still needs individualized curriculum as they pass through the last stages of egocentricity. Need leeway and encouragement to learn to understand and manage their own behavior.	• Eager to please.
• Crying less frequent, shorter in duration, and sometimes can be held back.
• Crying or physically aggressive behavior still emerge if verbal communication fails.
• Proud of being big but also aware that they are not yet "big kids." Easily shamed by correction; gentle and subtle reminders delivered as a secret are diplomatic ways to offer guidance.	• 5½ may bring an abrupt onset of temper tantrums, crying at routines, excitement, and fatigue.
• Generally stable and well-adjusted but still may hold some unreasonable fears.
• Interested in power and control: superhero, good guys/bad guys play.	

EMOTIONAL CONTROL (continued)

Younger Behavior	Older Behavior
• Spontaneous and reflexive actions cause child to hurt others without awareness; he will argue and deny the offence. Slowing down situations and verbalizing them can be helpful. • Increased social reciprocity and understanding, coupled with immature social skills and lack of experience, brings silly and boisterous interactions (chanting, bad words, name-calling, making faces) as children delight in their connection to one another. • Anxiety is seen in chewing on clothing, lip, hair, fidgeting, showing off, getting excited, and forgetting to pay attention. • May be selfish, impatient, bossy, verbally aggressive and rough. • May whine and be demanding or withdraw and disassociate when he feels his needs are not being met.	• Stress and anxiety continue to be expressed through restlessness, nose-picking, nail-biting, thumb-sucking, scratching, throat clearing, picking at or chewing on clothes.

SOCIAL BEHAVIOR

Younger Behavior	Older Behavior
• More ideas lead to more sustained play; can play alone, but prefers to be with others. • Plays best in groups of two or four; more social skill needed to manage play in a group of three. • Knows the rules, but believes rules are to manage others. • Aware of the group dynamic and hierarchy. More interested in his playmate or group than in the activity. • Emotionally manipulative and will exclude other children in an effort to control them or others. • Egocentric; cares about others' feelings but does not consider them relevant to his personal needs or wants. • Responds to verbal direction, and fewer techniques are needed. • Responds to silly language and singing. • Resists authority. Argues that "my parents said I could ..." • More independent in general, and routines go smoothly.	• Organized and capable; greater number of children can play cooperatively. • Solitary play has almost dropped out, but the restful camaraderie of parallel play can still be seen. • Limited exchange of ideas in group play; planning can be more important than the play. • Quarrels less, but has become more adept at teasing and insulting peers. • Games with winners still too challenging, leading to cheating as everyone wants to win. • Avoids adult disapproval. Needs, asks for, and accepts adult direction. Asks permission. Very sensitive to reprimands. Generally amenable and docile. • Enjoys having his own school life away from home. • Friendships are stronger. • Sensitive to his status in the group. • Feels shame and disgrace. • Enjoys group projects.

SOCIAL BEHAVIOR (continued)

Younger Behavior	Older Behavior
• Can be bossy or domineering with other children. Does better with one other child or when supervised. • Seeks out friends, will "mother" a new or shy child. • Despite anti-social conduct, name-calling, negativism, child is deeply interested in socializing. Acculturation proceeds at a rapid rate. • Tattling, disputing, and quarreling offer teachable moments in social skill development. • Impulsive; weak internal control as the conscience is nascent. • Will embarrass and hurt others' feelings to study their reaction. • Wants to be big … and feels small and vulnerable; a lot of bluster. • Feels insulted and embarrassed by correction; accepts correction if done in "secret." • Conversations have a "collective monologue" feel; children talk more than they listen to others.	• Appeals to adults to settle disputes, but also handles the situation more effectively and realistically by himself than earlier. • Prefers playmates of his own age. • Does not insist on his own way and does not worry about the behavior of others.

Appendix 2
Play-Based Learning that Supports Academic Success

Note that these are all-inclusive lists; teachers will probably want to choose just 5–7 skills to highlight in each area of the classroom.

In the Art Area Children Learn
- Self-expression, symbolic thinking
- Self-regulation
- Aesthetics
- Hand–eye coordination
- Motor control
- Structure
- Order
- Procedures
- Self-help
- Self-care
- Imagination

In the Block and Math Areas Children Learn

- ➤ Vocabulary
- ➤ Sorting
- ➤ Ordering
- ➤ Counting
- ➤ Measuring
- ➤ Logic
- ➤ Estimating sets and amounts
- ➤ Units of measurement
- ➤ Problem solving imagination
- ➤ Continuity permanence
- ➤ One-to-one correspondence
- ➤ To build attention span

In the Manipulative Area Children Learn

- ➤ Hand–eye coordination
- ➤ Problem solving
- ➤ Attention span
- ➤ Small motor skills
- ➤ Estimating skills
- ➤ Logic
- ➤ Order
- ➤ Spatial awareness
- ➤ Cooperation
- ➤ Sorting
- ➤ Relationships with others
- ➤ Length and measurement
- ➤ Comparison
- ➤ Numerosity
- ➤ Symmetry and balance

In the Sensory Play Area Children Learn

- Self-soothing, re-centering
- Sensory integration
- Measuring
- Hand–eye coordination
- Social skills
- Emotional regulation
- Sizes and shapes
- Muscle control

In the Dramatic Play Area Children Learn

- Social skills
- Listening skills
- Hierarchy of roles
- Reciprocity of language
- To see things from someone else's perspective
- To develop a plot
- Play a role
- Small muscle control
- Ordering, sorting
- Speaking up for themselves
- Language
- Vocabulary
- Empathy
- Compassion
- Self-reliant
- Develop friendships
- Cooperate with others

In the Natural Science Area Children Learn

- ➢ Observation skills
- ➢ Provoke inquiry
- ➢ Manipulation
- ➢ Hand–eye coordination
- ➢ Sorting and ordering
- ➢ Test hypotheses
- ➢ Build scientific reasoning
- ➢ Study difference and same

In the Book and Literacy Centers Children Learn

- ➢ Practice pre and early reading
- ➢ Learning rules and procedures for handling books
- ➢ Practice focused attention in a group
- ➢ Self-regulate in quiet play
- ➢ Copy the teacher's reading
- ➢ Look at pictures
- ➢ Develop imagination
- ➢ Learn how to find information
- ➢ Social skills
- ➢ Self-control
- ➢ Listening skills
- ➢ Letters and numbers

Appendix 3

Suggested Additional Reading or Viewing

Teaching through Play

Jones, Elizabeth, and Gretchen Reynolds, *The Play's the Thing: Teachers' Roles in Children's Play*, New York: Teachers College Press, 1992.

Observation

Cohen, Dorothy, Virginia Stern, and Nancy Balaban, *Observing and Recording the Behavior of Young Children*, Fourth Edition, New York: Teachers College Press, 1997.

Weaving Academics into Play

Bainer, Claire, and Gail Myers, *Literacy in the Preschool Years: A Play Based Approach*, Oakland, CA: BlueSkies for Children, 2010. DVD available at www.blueskies4children.org.

Understanding Children and Development

Neville, Helen, and Diane Clark Johnson, *Temperament Tools*, Seattle, WA: Parenting Press, 1998.

Siegel, Daniel, and Tina Payne Bryson, *The Whole Brain Child: 12 Revolutionary Strategies to Nurture your Child's Developing Mind*, New York: Bantam Books, 2011.

Studies and Perspectives on Teaching Young Children

Bronson, Po, and Ashley Merryman, *NurtureShock: New Thinking about Children*, New York: Twelve, Hachette Book Group, 2009.

Carlsson-Paige, Nancy, Geralyn Bywater McLaughlin, and Joan Wolfsheimer Almon, *Reading Instruction in Kindergarten: Little to Gain and Much to Lose*, Alliance for Childhood Defending the Early Years Project, 2015. Available at allianceforchildhood.org.

Galinsky, Ellen, *Mind in the Making: Seven Essential Life Skills Every Child Needs*, New York: HarperCollins, 2010.

Glossary

Age-appropriate Suited to the child's level of development, offering just the right degree of challenge to attract the child's curiosity but remain achievable with some effort.

Concrete thinking Literal, black-and-white thinking with no exceptions, no abstraction.

Constructive play Play which engages children in positive exploration and/or interaction, constructing their own knowledge. Jean Piaget used this term to describe play that requires the child to incorporate new information into what she already understands about the world.

Divergent thinking The process of generating creative ideas to explore many possible solutions: typically spontaneous, free flowing, and non-linear.

Domain Each area of development, typically labeled Physical (both gross and fine motor), Social, Emotional, Language, Sensory Integration, Aesthetic, Cognitive.

Egocentric Seeing only one's own point of view. Young children are born knowing only about their own needs and wants, and gradually learn that others also have needs and feelings—adults help him learn to see the perspective of others as they mature. (Different meaning than when applied to an adult, where egocentricity implies conceit and selfishness.)

Guided play Play accompanied by teacher guidance through the arrangement of the play area, the materials made available, and the teacher's additions to the child's ideas by means of commentary, questions, information, or materials.

Play Activity which is freely chosen, self-structured, and self-directed.

Positive redirection Intentionally focusing a child on a new activity or more helpful means of interaction.

Scaffold Offering information or activities to a child which are appropriate to his current level of development but, with the teacher's help, will help him move to the next level.

Temperament Inborn traits that dictate each person's primal responses. A child who needs time to observe and adjust to a new situation has a "slow to warm up" temperament.

Whole child Refers to the interrelatedness of development across domains in young children, each domain affecting the development of the others.

Zone of proximal development The difference between what a child can manage on her own and what she can manage with the help of another. Closely tied to the concept of scaffolding; both of these concepts come from Vygotsky.